# The Front Page

## A Play in Three Acts

by Ben Hecht & Charles MacArthur

A SAMUEL FRENCH ACTING EDITION

## SAMUEL FRENCH

FOUNDED 1830

New York  Hollywood  London  Toronto

SAMUELFRENCH.COM

**ISBN  978-0-573-60912-1**          Printed in U.S.A.          **#449**

3

# THE FRONT PAGE

A play in three acts by Ben Hecht and Chas. Mac-Arthur. Produced by Jed Harris at the Times Square Theatre, New York, August 14, 1928.

## CAST OF CHARACTERS

WILSON, *American* .................. *Vincent York*
ENDICOTT, *Post* .................... *Allen Jenkins*
MURPHY, *Journal* ............. *Willard Robertson*
McCUE, *City Press* ............... *William Foran*
SCHWARTZ, *Daily News* .......... *Tammany Young*
KRUGER, *Journal of Commerce*
                            *—Joseph Spurin-Calleia*
BENSINGER, *Tribune* ............. *Walter Baldwin*
MRS. SCHLOSSER .................... *Violet Barney*
WOODENSHOES EICHORN .............. *Jay Wilson*
DIAMOND LOUIS ............... *Eduardo Ciannelli*
HILDY JOHNSON, *Herald Examiner* ...... *Lee Tracy*
JENNIE .......................... *Carrie Weller*
MOLLIE MALLOY ............... *Dorothy Stickney*
SHERIFF HARTMAN ............... *Claude Cooper*
PEGGY GRANT ................... *Frances Fuller*
MRS. GRANT ................... *Jessie Crommette*
THE MAYOR ..................... *George Barbier*
MR. PINCUS .................... *Frank Conlan*
EARL WILLIAMS ................... *George Leach*
WALTER BURNS ................. *Osgood Perkins*
CARL, a Deputy ............... *Matthew Crowley*
FRANK, a Deputy ..................... *Gene West*
A POLICEMAN ..................... *Larry Doyle*
A POLICEMAN ................. *George T. Fleming*

ACTS I, II and III.—The Press Room of the Criminal Courts Building, Chicago.

Staged by George S. Kaufman,

# The Front Page

## ACT ONE

SCENE: *The Scene is the press room of the Criminal Courts Building, Chicago. The room is octagonal, and the audience sees five sides of the octagon. On the down Right side are two high windows; further up stage, at an angle, are double doors; the rear wall, which runs parallel with the foots, has two tables against it, up Right Center against the wall, and Center sticking out into the room. The first has two telephones and a typewriter on it. The second, one telephone and a pile of papers. The next wall, against an angle, has a huge roll-top desk against it; then comes the final wall, down Left, in which is the door Left to the toilet. A long table is Right Center at an angle. There are chairs around it, and four phones on it. The roll-top desk also has a phone on it. Six of these phones communicate directly with various newspapers; Number 4 phone on large Center table is an outside phone, an extension of the switchboard in the Criminal Courts Building. There is a water cooler between the big desk and the toilet door.*

TIME: *It is eight-thirty at night. At the rise four men are playing poker around the big table. They are* MURPHY, *hardest of the hard-boiled;* ENDICOTT, *recently married and inclined to complain about the job;* SCHWARTZ, *with the sick wife in the hospital and two children who have to live with his sister, and* WILSON, *who once sold a piece to the "Mercury," and is thinking of trying a play. Down-*

5

*stage Left, playing a banjo and singing, is KRUGER, a chronic loafer. Leaning back in the swivel chair in front of the desk McCUE. His feet are up on a scrap basket, a telephone in his hand. KRUGER'S tune at the rise is "By the Light of the Silvery Moon."*

AT RISE: *As the Curtain rises, McCUE is jiggling the hook on his telephone, trying to attract the operator. The poker players are hard at it. The position of the players is MURPHY at the Left end of the table, WILSON on the downstage side on a stool, ENDICOTT up Right, SCHWARTZ up Left.*

ENDICOTT. Crack it for a dime.

SCHWARTZ. By me.

MURPHY. I stay.

WILSON. Me too.

SCHWARTZ. I'm behind again. I was even a couple of minutes ago.

WILSON. Papers?

ENDICOTT. Three.

MURPHY. Two.

WILSON. Three to the dealer.

McCUE. *(Into phone)* Kenwood three *four hundred.*

*(The PHONE on the table up Center rings—the outside connection.)*

SCHWARTZ. *(Throwing his hand in. To MURPHY)* Remember your draw, will you, Jim?

McCUE. *(Indicating the ringing phone)* Hey, take that, one of you guys. Ernie, you're not doing *anything.*

*(They pay no attention. KRUGER'S voice comes up a little higher.)*

ENDICOTT. *(Throws down his cards with vehemence)* God *damn* it!

McCue. *(In annoyance at their not answering the other phone)* Oh! *(Props one phone receiver against his ear; reaches over and answers the other phone.)*

Wilson. Who opened this?

Murphy. I did!

McCue. What's the matter with you guys? Are you all crippled or something? *(Into second phone)* Press room!

Wilson. I check.

McCue. *(As though he had not been heard the first time)* Criminal Court press room! *(Quickly gives attention to the first phone)* Hello Sarge—McCue. Hold the line a minute. *(Back to the second phone)* No, I told you it was the press room. *(Hangs up; takes the first phone again)*

Anything doing, Sarge?—All right. Thank you, Sarge. *(Hangs up.)*

Endicott. *(To the Players: takes McCue's "I told you it was the press room" as cue)* What are you waiting for? (McCue *is jiggling the receiver again.)*     *(Together.)*

Murphy. How'd I know you were out? Two Johns.

Wilson. *(Showing Queens)* Ladies. *(Takes pot.)*

(Endicott *prepares to deal.)*

McCue. *(In phone)* Robey four five hundred.

Schwartz. *(To Murphy)* What'd you draw in?

Murphy. I don't know. Ernie! Take that mouth organ in the can and play it!

*(The MUSIC swells a little in reply.)*

Endicott. These cards are like washrags.

Wilson. Let's chip in for a new deck.

Schwartz. These are good enough— I'm eighty cents out already!

McCue. *(In phone)* Is this the home of Mrs. F. D. Margolies?

Murphy. I'd like a deck with some aces in it.

McCue. *(Waving* Murphy *to be silent,* Kruger *also stops his music)* Jim! *(The poker game is silent for the next few speeches.* Endicott *is unobtrusively finishing the deal.* McCue *talks into the phone)* Now, Mrs. Margolies, this is Mr. McCue of the City News Bureau— City News Bureau—is it true, Madame, that you were the victim of a Peeping Tom?

Kruger. Ask her if she's worth peeping at?

Wilson. Has she got a friend?

McCue. Now, that ain't the right attitude to take, Madame. All we want is the facts— Well, what did this Peeping Tom look like? I mean, for instance, would you say he looked like a college professor?

Endicott. Tell her I can run up for an hour.

Schwartz. Pass.

McCue. Just a minute, *Madame.* Is it true, Mrs. Margolies, that you took the part of Pocahontas in the Elks' Pageant seven years ago?—Hello. *(To the* Others*)* She hung up!

Murphy. The hell *with her!* A dime.

*(The ALARM sounds.)*

Endicott. *(When alarm is over)* Where's that fire?

Wilson. Three-two-one!

Schwartz. Clark and Eric.

Kruger. Too far. *(Starts playing and singing again.)*

McCue. *(Into phone)* Harrison four thousand.

Wilson. *(Throwing in his hand)* Drop.

Endicott. Stay.

Schwartz. *(Throwing down his hand. Wearily rises; stretches; ambles over and looks out the window. Speaks as he rises)* Oh, cripes!—what time is it, anyway?

*(The MUSIC becomes low.)*

WILSON. About half past eight. *(Rises.)*

MURPHY. *(Drawing cards)* One off the top.

WILSON. *(Crossing Left for a drink)* How's the wife, Ed? Any better?

SCHWARTZ. Worse.

WILSON. That's tough.

SCHWARTZ. Sitting here all night, waiting for them to hang Earl Williams. *(A gesture out the window.)*

KRUGER. *(Lazily)* It's hard work, all right.

McCUE. Hello, Sarge? McCue. (ENDICOTT *is giving himself two cards; squeezing his cards with interest)* Anything doing?

MURPHY. Dime!

ENDICOTT. Call.

McCUE. Yeah? That's swell. *(His tone makes the other PLAYERS pause; they ALL give attention. KRUGER stops strumming. WILSON, a glass of water at his lips, does not drink)* A love triangle, huh? *(Starts making notes)* Did he kill her?—Killed 'em both! Ah! Was she good-looking? *(A second of silence from EVERYONE)* What? Oh, Niggers!

ENDICOTT. Your deal, Ed! ⎤

(SCHWARTZ *crosses to his* ⎬ *(Together.)*
*chair.)* |

MURPHY. Aw! ⎦

*(They ALL relax.)*

KRUGER. That's a *break.*

*("Examiner" PHONE rings. It is on the main table. ENDICOTT answers.)*

McCUE. No, never mind—thank you, Sarge. *(Jiggles receiver)* Englewood, six eight hundred.

ENDICOTT. Criminal Court press room.

WALTER'S VOICE. Hildy Johnson there?

ENDICOTT. No. Hildy Johnson ain't here.

WALTER'S VOICE. Cut the stalling and put that son-ofabitch on the wire.

ENDICOTT. Oh, hello, Mr. Burns. *(MUSIC stops)* He ain't been in yet.

WALTER'S VOICE. You tell that dumb bastard if he knows what's good for him to call me up—

ENDICOTT. O.K. *(Hangs up)* Walter Burns again. Something must have happened.

SCHWARTZ. *(As he starts a deal)* I'm telling you what's happened. Hildy quit.

MURPHY. What do you mean, quit? He's a fixture on the *Examiner.*

KRUGER. Yeh. He goes with the woodwork.

WILSON. *(Crossing down Right to stool)* They're the journaleese twins.

ENDICOTT. You couldn't drag him away from Walter.

SCHWARTZ. All right, but that's what's happened, all right! I got it from Bert Neeley. I'm telling you— Hildy's gettin' married.

MURPHY. Hell, Walter wouldn't let him get married. He'd kidnap him at the altar.

McCUE. Hello, Sarge. McCue. Anything doing?

ENDICOTT. Remember what he did to Bill Fenton, when he wanted to go to Hollywood? Had him thrown in jail for arson.

MURPHY. Forgery.

McCUE. Shut up!— *(In phone)* Anybody hurt?— Oh, fine! What's his name?—Spell it— *(Starts to write name)* S—C—Z—J—Oh, the hell with it. *(Throws pencil away and jiggles receiver.)*

ENDICOTT. A guy ain't going to walk out on a job when he's drawing down seventy bucks a week.

SCHWARTZ. Answer me this one. If Hildy ain't quit, why ain't he here covering the hanging?

McCUE. *(In phone)* Give me rewrite. ⎫
WILSON. Aw! Walter would have sent ⎬ *(Together.)*
somebody in his place. ⎭

SCHWARTZ. *Something* must have happened, or what's he calling up all the time?

ENDICOTT. He sounded like he was having a hemorrhage.

McCUE. *(Into phone)* Hello, Emil. Nothing new on the hanging. But here's a great big scoop for you.

SCHWARTZ. *(Throwing down his hand)* I wish to God *I* could quit.

KRUGER. You'd think he'd come in and say goodbye.

MURPHY. Can't tell about that Swede. He's a crazy son-of-a—

McCUE. *(Taking cue, "Tell about that Swede")* Shut up, fellas— Ready, Emil? Dr. Irving Zobel—Z for Zebra—O for onion—B for baptize—E for anything and L for lousy—

MURPHY. Pass.

WILSON. By me.

ENDICOTT. Crack it for a dime.

(SCHWARTZ *tosses in his hand.*)

*(Through McCUE's speech.)*

MURPHY. Stay.

WILSON. Stay.

McCUE. *(An unbroken speech)* Yes, Zobel! That's right! With offices at sixteen-o-eight Cottage Grove Avenue. Well, this bird was arrested tonight on complaint of a lot of angry husbands. They claim he was treating their wives with electricity for a dollar a whack.

MURPHY. Is the Electric Teaser in again?

McCUE. *(In phone)* He had a big following, a regular army of fat old dames that was being neglected by their husbands. So they was visiting this Dr. Zobel in their kimonas to get electricity.

ENDICOTT. I understand he massages them too.

McCUE. *(In phone)* Anyhow, the Doctor is being held for malpractice and the station is full of his *patients* who claim he's innocent. But from what the husbands say it looks like he's a Lothario. All right. *(Hangs up; jiggles receiver.)*

MURPHY. Hey, Ernie, why don't you go in for electricity instead of the banjo?

(BENSINGER *enters up Right with a large roll of cotton and a book.)*

KRUGER. It's got no future.

McCUE. Sheridan two thousand.

BENSINGER. *(As he crosses Left to desk)* What the hell, Mac? Is that the only telephone in the place?

McCUE. *(Rises and crosses up Center to table)* It's the only one with a mouthpiece on it.

MURPHY. *(Putting down his hand)* Read 'em and weep. *(Takes the pot. Prepares to deal.)*

BENSINGER. How many times have I got to tell you fellows to leave my phone alone? If you've got to talk through a mouthpiece go *buy* one, like I did. *(He throws the scrap basket down Left towards* KRUGER.) } *(Together.)*

MURPHY. Aw, shut up, Listerine.

McCUE. *(Sitting on table up Center. In phone)* Sheridan two thousand.

BENSINGER. I'm trying to keep this phone clean and I'm not going to have you fellows coughing and spitting in it either, or pawing it with your hands. } *(Together.)*

SCHWARTZ. What is this?—a hospital or something?

ENDICOTT. How's that pimple coming along?

BENSINGER. *(Pulling dirty underwear from desk drawer)* And you don't have to use this desk for a toilet.

McCUE. *(In phone)* Two thousand.

MURPHY. Yeah? Well, suppose you quit stinking up this place with your Goddam antiseptics!

BENSINGER. *(Pulling a pie out of the desk)* Ain't

you guys got any self-respect? *(He rises, puts pie disgustedly in scrap basket and sits down.)*

McCUE. *(In phone)* Hello! Sarge!—*McCue*—Congratulation on that Polack's capture, Sarge. I hear you're going to be promoted. Anything doing?

WILSON. *(Taking cue "Self-respect")* Nickel.

ENDICOTT. Up a dime.

SCHWARTZ. Drop.

MURPHY. *(Throwing down his hand)* Aw!

WILSON. Stay. *(The dealing starts.* BENSINGER *takes a soda mint tablet.)*

McCUE. *(A continuous speech)* Yeah—Just a second, Sarge? *(To the* PLAYERS*)* Nice little feature, fellas. Little kid, golden curls, everything, lost out near Grand Crossing. The cops are feeding her candy.

(BENSINGER *starts spraying his phone.)*

MURPHY. Is that all?

McCUE. Don't you want **it?**

SCHWARTZ. No!

ENDICOTT. Stick it!

KRUGER. I don't want *anything.*

WILSON. All yours. *(Starts to deal a new hand.)*

McCUE. Never mind, Sarge. Thank you, Sarge. (McCUE *hangs up, gets up, crosses Left for a drink.)*

*(Together.)*

WILSON. I'm all through drawing to flushes.

SCHWARTZ. Anything new on the hanging, Bensinger?

WILSON. *(Dealing)* My deal, isn't it?

MURPHY. Hey! Zenita!

BENSINGER. *(Wiping phone with his handkerchief)* What is it?

MURPHY. Question before the house: Gentleman wants to know what's new on the hanging.

BENSINGER. Nothing special.

KRUGER. *(With a yawn)* Did you see the Sheriff?

BENSINGER. Why don't you get your own news?

KRUGER. Somebody ought to see the Sheriff.

ENDICOTT. Anyhow, this looks like the last hanging we'll ever have to cover. I open.

SCHWARTZ. Yah. Can you imagine their putting in an electric chair? That's awful.

ENDICOTT. Going to toast them, like Lucky Strikes.

MURPHY. Who opened?

SCHWARTZ. What's the matter? Got a hand? *(Throws his away.)*

MURPHY. Up a dime.

WILSON. Stay.

ENDICOTT. Stay. Three cards.

(MRS SCHLOSSER *enters up Right.)*

MURPHY. I'll play these.

SCHWARTZ. I thought so.

(MRS. MYRTLE SCHLOSSER *takes a quick look around. Not a great deal of attention is paid to her, but enough to cause the* BOYS *to look at her, and thus hold the game for a few seconds.)*

ENDICOTT. Hello, Mrs. Schlosser. Herman hasn't been in yet.

McCUE. *(Crossing Center)* Hello, Mrs. Schlosser. Have you tried the Harrison Street Station? He may be sleeping in the squad room.

MRS. SCHLOSSER. *(Crossing down Center)* You don't say?

SCHWARTZ. What became of that rule about women coming into this press room?

MURPHY. Yeah—I don't let my *own* wife come in here.

MRS. SCHLOSSER. Did he have any money left when you saw him?

McCUE. *(Reading paper)* Well, I didn't exactly see him. Did you, Mike?

ENDICOTT. No, I didn't really see him either.

MRS. SCHLOSSER. Oh, you didn't? Well, was he still drinking?

McCUE. I tell you what, I'll call up the grand jury room if you want. Sometimes he goes to sleep up there.

MRS. SCHLOSSER. Don't trouble yourself! I notice Hildy Johnson ain't here either. I suppose the two of them are out sopping it up together.

SCHWARTZ. Now, you mustn't talk that way, Mrs. Schlosser. Hildy's reformed—he's gettin' married.

MRS. SCHLOSSER. Married? Well, all I can say is, God help his wife!

MURPHY. Come on—are we playing cards or aren't we?

MRS. SCHLOSSER. I suppose you've cleaned Herman out.

WILSON. Honest, Mrs. Schlosser, we ain't seen him.

MRS. SCHLOSSER. *(Bitterly)* He can't come home. I kept dinner waiting till eleven o'clock last night and he never even *called up*.

ENDICOTT. Well, why pick on us?

*(PHONE rings.)*

KRUGER. Yeh—we're busy.

ENDICOTT. *(In phone)* Press room.

MRS. SCHLOSSER. *(Crossing Left)* You know where he is, you're just covering up for him.

WALTER'S VOICE. Is that stinking Swede there yet?

ENDICOTT. No, Mr. Burns, Hildy ain't showed up yet.

MRS. SCHLOSSER. *(Stops)* Is that Walter Burns? Let me talk to him— *(She crosses Right.)*

ENDICOTT. *(Taking cue "talk to him")* Just a minute, Mr. Burns. Herman Schlosser's wife wants to talk to you. *(Gives her phone.)*

MURPHY. *(Simultaneously)* Come on. Who opened?

ENDICOTT. Check it—

MURPHY. A dime—

WALTER'S VOICE. *(Continuous speech. Continuing through the foregoing)* There's no use pretending that lousy Swede ain't there—cause I can hear him—Johnson—Who?

MRS. SCHLOSSER. *(In phone. Taking cue "to talk to you")* Hello, Mr. Burns. This is Mrs. Schlosser.

WALTER'S VOICE. Do you see Hildy Johnson around anywhere?

MRS. SCHLOSSER. No, Mr. Burns.

WALTER'S VOICE. Well, how are you—

MRS. SCHLOSSER. Oh, I'm very well thank you. Mr. Burns, I was just wondering if you knew where Herman was— He didn't come home last night and it was pay day—

WALTER'S VOICE. Forget it. It'll be all right.

MRS. SCHLOSSER. But it won't be all right, I'm just going crazy—

WALTER'S VOICE. Well why don't you come down early and collect his pay like everybody else.

*(The game continues with looks from* REPORTERS.*)*

MRS. SCHLOSSER. Well I have done that but the cashier won't give it to me, and I was just wondering could you give me some kind of an order.

WALTER'S VOICE. Sure. Drop in anytime.

MRS. SCHLOSSER. Oh, will you? That's awfully good of you—

WALTER'S VOICE. Nothing at all— Goodbye.

MRS. SCHLOSSER. You know I hate to do a thing like that— But you know how Herman is about money.

WALTER'S VOICE. I know— Just a God damn bum—

MRS. SCHLOSSER. Thank you ever so much— *(Hangs up; turns on the* REPORTERS*)* You're all alike, everyone of you!

MURPHY. *(To* WILSON, *the next player)* What do you do, Jack?

MRS. SCHLOSSER. You ought to be ashamed of yourselves!

MURPHY. *(To* MRS. SCHLOSSER) All right, we're ashamed. *(To* WILSON) A dime's bet.

MRS. SCHLOSSER. *(Crossing Center above* MURPHY*)* Sitting around like a lot of tramps! Drinking and bumming! Poker! *(She grabs* MURPHY's *cards and backs up Right.)*

MURPHY. *(Leaping up in fury)* Here! Gimme those! What the hell!

*(MUSIC stops.)*

MRS. SCHLOSSER. You know where he is, and I'm going to stay right here till I find out.

MURPHY. Well, he's at Hockstetter's, that's where he is! Now give me those cards!

MRS. SCHLOSSER. Where?

WILSON. The Turkish Bath on Madison Street!

ENDICOTT. In the basement!

MURPHY. Now give me those!

MRS. SCHLOSSER. So! You did know. (MURPHY *nervously awaiting his cards)* Dirty liars. *(Throws them face up on the table.)*

MURPHY. *(As she throws them)* Hey!

*(They spread out on the table.)*

MRS. SCHLOSSER. *(Crossing up Center)* A fine bunch of gentlemen, I must say! Newspapermen! Bums! *(She exits.)*

*(*SCHWARTZ *and* WILSON *grasp their foreheads as they see the hand.)*

MURPHY. *(Crossing Center back of his chair)* Look! The second straight flush I ever held.

*(*BENSINGER *picks up phone.)*

ENDICOTT. Jese!

MURPHY. *(Pointing to cards)* Eight, nine, ten, jack, and queen of spades. *(He sits)* If I was married to that dame I'd kick her humpbacked.

BENSINGER. City desk!

WILSON. Tough luck. I don't think I'd have called, anyhow.

ENDICOTT. *(Gathering the cards together)* I don't know what gets into women. I took Bob Brody home the other night and his wife broke his arm with a broom, and not only that—

*(BENSINGER has interrupted. ENDICOTT continues the story in a whisper.)*

BENSINGER. *(Taking cue "broom," has collected his notes)* Shut up, you guys! *(Into phone. MCCUE sits on table and starts to do a crossword puzzle)* This is Bensinger. Here's a new lead on the Earl Williams hanging— Yeah, I just saw the Sheriff. He won't move the hanging up a minute— I don't care *who* he promised— All right, I'll talk to him again, but it's no use. The execution is set for seven o'clock in the morning.

*(ENDICOTT starts to deal.)*

KRUGER. *(To the tune of "Three O'clock in the Morning," sings)* Seven o'clock in the morning.

BENSINGER. *(Takes cue "seven o'clock")* Shut up, Ernie— *(In phone)* Give me a rewrite man.

KRUGER. Why can't they jerk these guys at a reasonable hour, so we can get some sleep.

BENSINGER. *(To KRUGER)* I asked the Sheriff to move it up to five, so we could make the City Edition. Just because I asked him to, he wouldn't.

MURPHY. That guy wouldn't do anything for his mother.

KRUGER. He gives a damn if we stay up all night. *(KRUGER puts banjo under chair.)*

ENDICOTT. You've got no kick coming. Look at me! I've had two dinners home in the last month. Worked on my day off three weeks running.

BENSINGER. *(Into phone)* Hello. Jake?—New lead on the Earl Williams hanging. (ENDICOTT *stops in the middle of the deal. The* REPORTERS *listen)* Ready? —The condemned man ate a hearty dinner·— Yeah, mock turtle soup, chicken pot pie, *(Looks at notes)* hashed brown potatoes, combination salad, and pie a la mode.

KRUGER. Make mine the same.

BENSINGER. No—I don't know *what* kind of pie.

MURPHY. Eskimo!

MCCUE. I wish I had a hamburger sandwich.

BENSINGER. And, Jake, get this in as a big favor. The whole dinner was furnished by Charlie Apfel— Yeah—Apfel. A for adenoids, P for psychology, F for Frank, E for Eddie and L for—ah—

MURPHY. Lay an egg.

BENSINGER. Proprietor of the "Apfel-Wants-To-See-You"-restaurant.

ENDICOTT. *(Has finished dealing)* That means a new hat for *somebody.*

SCHWARTZ. You lousy grafter.

MURPHY. *(Rising and crossing Right Center)* I better catch the fudge, fellas. *(Back of table)* Is it open?

*(The next few poker speeches run through* BENSINGER'S *next speech.)*

SCHWARTZ. *(After a beat)* Nickel.

MURPHY. *(After two beats)* Stay. *(Crosses, picks up phone.)*

WILSON. Drop.

ENDICOTT. Stay— Cards?

SCHWARTZ. Three.

(MURPHY *pantomimes for three.)*

BENSINGER. *(Taking* MURPHY's *"fudge, fellas" as his cue)* Now here's the situation on the eve of the hanging. The officials are prepared for a general uprising of radicals at the hour of execution, but the Sheriff still refuses to be intimidated by the Red menace.

MURPHY. *(Into his phone, while pantomiming for three cards)* Give me a rewrite man, will you?

ENDICOTT. Three for me!

MURPHY. —Yeah. Some more bunk on the Earl Williams hanging.

BENSINGER. *(Into phone, as the* REPORTERS *all listen)* A double guard has just been thrown around the jail, the municipal buildings, railroad terminals, and elevated stations. Also, the Sheriff has just received four more letters threatening his life.

MURPHY. Hurry up, will you?

BENSINGER. He's going to answer these threats by a series of raids against the Friends of American Liberty and other Bolshevik organizations. Call you later. *(He hangs up.)*

SCHWARTZ. *(Taking cue "threatening his life")* Bet a dime.

MURPHY. *(Into phone)* Ready?—Sheriff Hartman has just put two hundred more relatives on the payroll to protect the city against the Red Army, which is leaving Moscow in a couple of minutes *(Consults his hand, speaks in an aside)* Up a dime. *(Back to phone)* And to prove to the voters that the Red menace is on the square, he has just wrote himself four more letters threatening his life. I know he wrote them on account of the misspelling.

ENDICOTT. Drop.

MURPHY. That's all, except the doomed man ate a hearty dinner. As follows: Noodle soup, rusta-biff, sweet a potat', cranberry sauce, a pie-a-a-ala mud.

SCHWARTZ. I raise another dime.

MURPHY. *(Consults his cards)* Wait a minute. Up again. *(Back to phone)* Statement from who? The

Sheriff?—Quote him for anything you want to—he can't *read. (Hangs up.)*

(BENSINGER's *PHONE rings instantly.)*

SCHWARTZ. Call.

MURPHY. *(Crossing Center)* **Three** bullets. Pay at this window.

BENSINGER. Hello.

WILSON. Shuffle that deck. I get the same hand every time.

(MURPHY *sits.)*

BENSINGER. What? *(To* MCCUE *as* SCHWARTZ *starts to shuffle)* For God's sake, didn't you send that in about the new alienist?

MCCUE. I got my hands full with the stations.

BENSINGER. *(Into phone)* All right, I'll give you what I got. *(He looks at notes)* Dr. Max J. Egglehoffer. From Vienna. There's a dozen envelopes on him in the morgue— Well, he's going to examine Williams at the request of—ah—wait a minute— *(Shuffles through his notes)* —the request of the United Federation for World Betterment.

KRUGER. I'm for that.

BENSINGER. Sure—one of the biggest alienists in the world. He's the author of that book, "The Personality Gland."

MCCUE. *(Still at the crossword puzzle)* And where to put it.

BENSINGER. He just autographed it for me.

MURPHY. Did he bite his initials in your pants, too? —Nickel.

KRUGER. Give me the City desk!

WILSON. Drop.

ENDICOTT. Drop.

SCHWARTZ. Drop.

MURPHY. Ah! *(Gathers the cards together; shuffles.)*

BENSINGER. *(At phone still)* All right. He's going to examine him in about fifteen minutes. I'll let you know. *(Hangs up.)*

KRUGER. Kruger calling! Nothing new on the hanging.

*(McCUE stirs himself, goes to small table up Center. BENSINGER reading "The Personality Gland.")*

SCHWARTZ. Say, how about roodles on our straights or better? I want to get some of my dough back.

*(KRUGER gets up lazily, crosses up Center. Lights cigarette.)*

WILSON. Hey, I thought we weren't going to give them alienists any more free advertising.

*(McCUE takes up the phone on the small table.)*

ENDICOTT. That's the fourteenth pair of whiskers they called in on this God damned case.

MURPHY. Ah, they make me sick. All these alienists do is goose you and send you a bill for five-hundred bucks.

McCUE. *(Into phone)* This is McCue— Looks like the hanging's coming off at seven all right— Yeah, the Governor's gone fishing and can't be found— No, fishing. Yeah—that's *right*. *(From the courtyard comes the whir and CRASH of a gallows being tested)* They're testing the gallows now— Yeah. Testing 'em with sandbags— Maybe you can hear 'em. *(Holds up phone toward window and laughs)* What? The same to you. *(Hangs up.)*

SCHWARTZ. I wish to God they'd quit practicing.

WILSON. *(Tossing in a coin)* Crack it!

KRUGER. *(Crossing Right and yelling out of window)* Hey, Jacobi! Quit playing with that gallus! How do you expect us to do any work?

VOICE. *(From jail yard)* Cut that yelling, you bums!
McCUE. Ain't much respect for the press around here.

*(The FIRE ALARM sounds same number as before. Through it runs the following poker talk.)*

ENDICOTT. Drop.
SCHWARTZ. Stay.
MURPHY. Drop. How many, Jack?
WILSON. One.
SCHWARTZ. Two.
MURPHY. Bet 'em up.
McCUE. That's a second alarm, ain't it?
MURPHY. Who cares?
McCUE. Not me.
KRUGER. *(Without stirring)* Probably some orphanage.
MURPHY. Maybe it's another cat-house. Remember when Big Minnie's burned down, and the Mayor at Galesburg came *running out.*

*(PHONE on McCUE's table rings.)*

WILSON. Dime.
SCHWARTZ. I call.
WILSON. Two sixes.
SCHWARTZ. Aw, trying to steal one, eh?
McCUE. *(At phone)* What? The Mayor's office. May be a statement.
KRUGER. Tell 'em we're busy.
McCUE. Hello. Hello, you God damned Swede! *(To* REPORTERS) It's Hildy.
MURPHY. What's he doing in the Mayor's office?
McCUE. What? What's that? What? He's stinko! What are you doing with the Mayor?
MURPHY. If he's got any left tell him to bring it over.
McCUE. Huh? Kissing him goodbye?

ENDICOTT. Tell him to come over and kiss us.

MURPHY. Tell him I'm getting ready.

McCUE. Well, hurry up. *(He hangs up)* He's stepping high.

MURPHY. What did he say?

KRUGER. Is he coming over?

McCUE. That's what he said.

*(WOODENSHOES EICHORN enters up Right. He is a big, moon-faced, optimistic, impressionable German cop.)*

ENDICOTT. Pass.

SCHWARTZ. By.

MURPHY. Me.

WILSON. Take a deal.

BENSINGER. Hello, Woodenshoes.

WOODENSHOES. *(Crossing down Center)* Say! I just been over to the death house!

BENSINGER. That so? Got any news?

WOODENSHOES. Yes, Mr. Bensinger, I have. Did you hear what Earl Williams said to the priest?

ENDICOTT. Aw, forget it.

MURPHY. The paper's so full of the hanging now we ain't got room for the ads.

BENSINGER. What did he say, Woodenshoes?

WOODENSHOES. He says to the priest that he was innocent.

MURPHY. Do you know any more jokes?

WOODENSHOES. Well, I'm just telling you what he says.

MURPHY. I suppose that copper committed suicide. Or maybe it was a love pact.

WOODENSHOES. Well, Williams has got a very good explanation for that.

ENDICOTT. *(As he deals)* Why don't you cry over him? Why don't you send him some roses like Mollie Malloy?

SCHWARTZ. Yeah. She thinks he's innocent too.

WOODENSHOES. *(To Center table)* You fellas don't understand. He admits killing the policeman, but he claims they're just using that as an excuse to hang him on account he's a radical. *(To* McCUE*)* But the thing that gets me—

McCUE. Before you go on, Woodenshoes, would you mind running down to the corner and getting me a hamburger sandwich.

WOODENSHOES. Personally, my feeling is that Earl Williams is a dual personality type on account of the way his head is shaped. *(He moves up above* MURPHY's *chair)* It's a typical case of psychology.

MURPHY. Three.

WILSON. One.

WOODENSHOES. Now you take the events leading up to the crime; his hanging a red flag out of the window on Washington's Birthday. That ain't normal, to begin with. The officer ought to have realized when he went up there that he was dealing with a lunatic. *(He crosses towards* ENDICOTT*)* And I'll tell you why—

ENDICOTT. Make that two hamburgers, will you, Woodenshoes, like a good fellow?

(WILSON *signals for one too.)*

WOODENSHOES. *(Crossing Center)* I thought you fellas might be interested in the psychological end of it. None of the papers have touched on it.

MURPHY. Listen, Woodenshoes, this guy Williams is just a bird that had the tough luck to kill a nigger policeman in a town where the nigger vote is important.

*(During the rest of scene* WOODENSHOES *watches each speaker with his lips moving in corroboration.)*

KRUGER. Sure! If he'd bumped him off down south they'd have given him a banquet and a trip to Europe.

MURPHY. Say, Williams was a bonanza for that City

Hall outfit. He gets hung—everybody gets elected on a law and order platform.

ENDICOTT. "Reform the Reds with a Rope."

WILSON. *(Derisively)* Hah!

MURPHY. When that baby drops through the trap tomorrow, it's a million votes. He's just a divine accident. Bet a dime.

WOODENSHOES. That's it, Mr. Murphy, an accident. *(He turns to* McCUE*)* Why, when this officer woke him up—

McCUE. Sure. You're right, Woodenshoes. And ask 'em to put a lot of ketchup on one of them sandwhiches, will you?

*(DIAMOND LOUIE enters up Right.)*

WILSON. *(Throws down his hand. He rises and crosses Right to lower window)* I haven't filled a hand all night.

LOUIE. *(Crossing behind* SCHWARTZ*)* Hello, fellows.

*(WOODENSHOES backs up Center.)*

SCHWARTZ. Diamond Louie!

MURPHY. Oooh! Look at the pop bottles!

McCUE. Hurry up, Woodenshoes! I'm starving!

KRUGER. Get one for me, Woodenshoes!

BENSINGER. Make mine a plain lettuce—on gluten bread.

WOODENSHOES. Where am I gonna get the dough for all these eats?

McCUE. Charge it.

MURPHY. You got a badge, ain't you? What's it good for?

WOODENSHOES. *(Shuffling out)* Four hamburgers and a lettuce.

McCUE. *(Calling after)* And a slice of onion!

LOUIE. *(Has been standing, reserved and silent, smoking. Casually, to the* PLAYERS*)* Who's ahead?

MURPHY. I'm out two bucks.

ENDICOTT. Listen to him! He's a big winner, Louie.

LOUIE. Where's Hildy? Ain't he in the game?

ENDICOTT. Sure he is! Can't you see? *(He points to* WILSON'S *empty stool.)*

KRUGER. Say, Louie. I hear your old gang is going to bump off Kinky White.

LOUIE. *(Crossing Center)* Is that so?

MURPHY. Better wait till after election or you won't get on the front page.

ENDICOTT. Yeah—we had to spike that Willie Mercer killing.

LOUIE. Well, I tell you, I don't associate with them fellows any more.

MURPHY. Go on—you got to kill somebody every day or you don't get any supper.

LOUIE. All jokin' aside—honest. I'm one of you fellows now. I'm in the newspaper game.

MURPHY. You're what?

ENDICOTT. Yeah! He's got delusions of grandeur.

LOUIE. *(Pointing at* ENDICOTT *and nodding)* Yeah, that's right. I'm a newspaper man. Workin' for Walter Burns.

WILSON. What?

ENDICOTT. What are you doing for Walter—writing the society colmun?

MURPHY. He's a marble editor.

LOUIE. I'm assistant circulation manager for the North Side. *(Walks up Center.)*

WILSON. Got a title and everything.

ENDICOTT. Burns will be hiring animal acts next.

SCHWARTZ. What did I tell you?—Walter sent him over to dig up Hildy. Didn't he?

MURPHY. That's why you're sucking around?

ENDICOTT. Chasing Hildy, huh?

WILSON. Say, what do you know about that, Louie? We heard he quit the *Examiner.*

(LOUIE *turns to* REPORTERS.)

McCue. Yeah, what's the dope, Louie?

Wilson. Did he?

Louie. Well, I don't think it's permanent.

Schwartz. What the hell happened?

Endicott. They must have murdered each other, the way Walter sounded.

Louie. Na-a-a. Just a little personal argument. Do you know what I mean? *(He crosses Right putting out cigarette on floor.)*

McCue. Give us the low-down.

Schwartz. Didn't I tell you he quit?

Louie. I don't know a thing about it.

McCue. Shall I tell Hildy you were looking for him?

Louie. No, *never mind. (Again the WHIR and CRASH of the gallows.* Louie *crosses to window)* What's that?

Endicott. They're fixing up a pain in the neck for somebody.

Louie. Ah, Mr. Williams.

Murphy. They'll be doing that for you some day.

Louie. *(Smiling as he turns)* Maybe— *(He crosses Center)* Well, keep your eye on the dealer—

Murphy. *(Leaning back in chair)* Wait a second, Louie— (Louie *stops)* Come here— (Louie *comes down just above* Murphy) Where do you carry your cap pistol?—Here? *(He gooses* Louie.)

Louie. *(Leaping as the* Boys *laugh)* Hey, for God's sake, look out. *(He crosses up Center. He turns to them)* That's a hell of a thing. *(Exits up Right, buttoning coat.)*

Endicott. Call again, Louie.

Murphy. Anytime you're in the building.

Kruger. *(Picking up banjo)* Don't bump anybody off before election, Louie!

Murphy. Louie hasn't got much self-control.

McCue. He's no boob. He's bumped off plenty. Louie has.

Kruger. Plenty of what?

ENDICOTT. What do you know about Hildy? Looks like he quit all right.

WILSON. Yeah—what do you think of that?

ENDICOTT. Well, there won't be any good reporters left after a while.

MURPHY. No. Mossie Enright getting stewed and falling down that elevator shaft. And poor old Larry *Malm.*

*(TELEPHONE rings.)*

SCHWARTZ. And Carl Pancake that disappeared.

ENDICOTT. *(In phone)* Hello.

WALTER'S VOICE. Did that bastard come in yet?

ENDICOTT. Oh, hello, Mr. Burns.

WALTER'S VOICE. Did Hildy Johnson come in yet?

ENDICOTT. Why, he was in the Mayor's office a few minutes ago—

WALTER'S VOICE. Mayor's office? Now God damn it!

ENDICOTT. Yeah, he just called up.

HILDY. *(Enters up Right. He carries a cane)* Sound your A, kid— *(He slides his suitcase to* KRUGER *and crosses down Left.)*

ENDICOTT. Wait a minute!

MURPHY. Ooooh. Look at the cane. What are you doing? Turning fairy?

McCUE. Oooh. Kiss me.

WILSON. Where the hell you been?

McCUE. What's the matter, Hildy? You got a shave.

SCHWARTZ. Look at the crease in his pants.

WALTER'S VOICE. *(Continuous speech)* I wanna talk to that lousy God damn Swede right now, and I'm not going to take any stalling.

ENDICOTT. *(Rising. Covering receiver)* It's Walter Burns. Will you talk to him for God's sake—

HILDY. *(Turning to* REPORTERS*)* Tell that paranoic to take a sweet kiss for himself. Come on, Ernie. *(Sings)* "Goodbye Forever."

ENDICOTT. Say listen, Hildy, will you do us a favor and talk to him? He knows you're here.

McCUE. He's called up nine million times.

(HILDY *stabs* MURPHY *with cane.*)

MURPHY. What's the matter? Scared of him?

HILDY. I'll talk to the maniac. I'll talk to him with the greatest of pleasure. *(He crosses Right.* ENDICOTT *backs up Right, taking his cane)* Hello, Mr. Burns.

WALTER'S VOICE. You dirty double crossing Swede—

HILDY. What's that, Mr. Burns?

WALTER'S VOICE. You double crossing sonofabitch.

HILDY. Why your language is shocking, Mr. Burns.

WALTER'S VOICE. Walking out on me like a stinkin' yellow belly.

HILDY. Now listen, you lousy baboon. Get a pencil and paper and take this down. Get this straight because this is important, Mr. Burns. It's the Hildy Johnson curse—

WALTER'S VOICE. You two-faced bastard!

HILDY. The next time I see you, no matter where I am, or what I'm doing I'm going to walk right up to you and hammer on that monkey skull of yours till it rings like a Chinese gong—

McCUE. Oh boy—

ENDICOTT. That's telling him.

WALTER'S VOICE. You God damn tittering Swede moron—you lousy stewbum.

HILDY. Listen to him! *(Holds out receiver.)*

WALTER'S VOICE. You're going to cover the hanging like I asked you or by God—

HILDY. No I ain't going to cover the hanging— I wouldn't cover the Last Supper for you—if they had it all over again in the middle of Clark Street—

WALTER'S VOICE. Hildy—honest to God—you're the only newspaperman I got on the staff.

HILDY. Never mind the vaseline, Jocko! It won't do you any good this time because I'm going to New York like I told you— And if you know what's good for you, you'll stay west of Gary, Indiana. A Johnson never forgets.

WALTER'S VOICE. Keep your shirt on— God damn it.

HILDY. *(He hangs up)* And that, boys, is what is known as telling the managing editor.

McCUE. I'll say it is!

MURPHY. What are you going to do? *(Together.)*

WILSON. What's the big idea?

BENSINGER. Can't you guys talk without yelling?

HILDY. *(He backs up Right singing)* "Goodbye Forever!"

VOICE. *(From yard)* Hey, cut out the yodeling! Where do you think you are!

HILDY. *(Moving toward window, taking out his pocket flask as he goes)* Hey, Jacobi! Pickle-*nose!* *(Throws it out the window.)*

VOICE. *(Outside)* Hey!

HILDY. *(Laughing) On* the button!

(KRUGER *puts down banjo.)*

BENSINGER. Shut up.

(HILDY *crosses up to* McCUE's *table and takes off overcoat and hat.)*

KRUGER. Come on now, let's have the low-down, Hildy?

WILSON. What did you quit for?

SCHWARTZ. We hear you're going to get married?

(ENDICOTT *sits on Right end of table Center.)*

McCUE. Yah! Are you getting married?

HILDY. You bet your life I'm getting married! *(Shows tickets)* See that? Three tickets to New York! Eleven-eighteen tonight!

WILSON. Tonight!

McCUE. Jese, that's quick!

HILDY. *(He takes off coat)* Me and my girl and her God damned Ma!

ENDICOTT. Kinda sudden, ain't it?

SCHWARTZ. What do you want to get married for?

HILDY. *(He takes off vest)* None of your damned business!

MURPHY. Oooooch! He's in love! Tootsie-wootsie!

(HILDY *starts down Center between* MURPHY *and* SCHWARTZ.)

McCUE. Is she a white girl?

ENDICOTT. Is she got a good shape?

WILSON. Does Walter know you're getting married?

HILDY. *(He starts to take off his shirt and tie)* Does Walter know I'm getting married? He congratulated me! Shook hands like a pal! Offered to throw me a farewell dinner!

ENDICOTT. That's his favorite joke—farewell dinners.

MURPHY. He poisons people at them.

HILDY. He gets me up to Polack Mike's—fills me full of rotgut— I'd have been there yet if it hadn't been for the fire escape!

SCHWARTZ. That's what he done to the Chief of Police!

HILDY. Can you imagine? Trying to bust up my marriage! After shaking hands!— *(He crosses Center)* Say, my girl didn't call up, did she, or come in looking for me? What time is it anyway?

SCHWARTZ. Quarter past nine.

HILDY. *(Crossing back to table, he opens parcel with clean shirt in it)* Nine? I got to be at this house at seven.

ENDICOTT. What house?

HILDY. Somebody giving a farewell party to my girl.

WILSON. At seven tonight?

HILDY. Yah!

MURPHY. You got to run like hell.

HILDY. *(Finishing taking off his shirt)* Oh, that's all right. Fellow doesn't quit a job every day. Especially when it's Walter Burns. The lousy baboon—

ENDICOTT. When's the wedding, Hildy?

HILDY. *(He starts up Right, turns, crosses to desk and puts shirt in drawer)* It's in New York, so you guys ain't going to have any fun with it. None of them fake warrants or kidnapping the bride, with me!

BENSINGER. Aw, for God's sake! *(Throws the shirt on the floor.)*

WILSON. Everybody's getting this New York bug. It's just a rube town.

SCHWARTZ. I was on a New York paper once—the *Times*. Jese! You might as well work in a bank.

MURPHY. I hear all the reporters in New York are lizzies.

McCUE. Remember that fellow from the *New York World?*

ENDICOTT. With the derby?

MURPHY. *(Presumably mimicking a New York journalist)* Could you please instruct me where the telegraph office is? You'll be talking like that, Hildy.

HILDY. Yah?

ENDICOTT. Which one of them sissy journals are you going to work for?

HILDY. None of them!

McCUE. *What?*

HILDY. *(Putting on shirt)* Who the hell wants to work on a newspaper? A lot of crumby hoboes, full of dandruff and bum gin they wheedle out of nigger Aldermen.

MURPHY. That's what comes of stealing a cane.

ENDICOTT. What are *you* going in for—the movies?

HILDY. *(Fairly sober now, and taking his time)* I am not. Advertising business. One hundred and fifty smackers a week.

McCUE. Yeah?

ENDICOTT. One hundred and fifty what? ⎫
MURPHY. Go tell Aunt Rhody! ⎭ *(Together.)*

SCHWARTZ. *(Thoughtfully)* A hundred and fifty.

HILDY. And here's the little old contract.

McCUE. *(Crossing Center.)* Let's see!

HILDY. *(Hands it to* McCUE, *who starts to look through it. Two or three of the* OTHERS *crowd around him)* I was just waiting to get it down in black and white before I walked in and told Walter I was through.

McCUE. *(With contract)* Jese, it is a hundred and fifty. *(Hands it back to* HILDY.)

WILSON. Was he sore?

ENDICOTT. What did Walter say?

HILDY. *(Tucking in his shirt)* The lousy snake-brain? The God damn ungrateful ape! Called me a traitor, after ten years of sweating my pants off for practically nothing. Traitor to what? What did he or anybody else in the newspaper business ever do for me except try to make a bum out of me! Says "you can't quit without notice!" What the hell does he think I am? A hired girl! Why, one more word and I'd have busted his whiskey snout for him!

KRUGER. Why didn't you?

MURPHY. Who's going to cover the hanging for the *Examiner?*

McCUE. Why didn't you tell us?

WILSON. Yah—instead of waiting till the last day?

HILDY. *(Crossing Left with necktie)* And have Walter hear about it? I've always wanted to walk in and quit just like that! *(A snap of the fingers)* I been planning this for two months—packed up *everything* yesterday, and so did my girl! Furniture and all. *(FIRE BELL has been sounding through the last few words. Number One-two-one.* HILDY *steps Center)* Hey, fellows, that Kenzie and Madison, ain't it? The Washington Irving School's out there.

MURPHY. Who's in school this time of night?

McCUE. What do you care, anyhow? You've quit.

HILDY. Just thought it might be a *good* fire, that's all.

*(Again the WHIR and CRASH of the gallows. HILDY crosses Left to mirror.)*

KRUGER. *(Rising and crossing Right to window)* For crying out loud! It's driving me crazy. Ain't you got anything else to do? Hey! You Jacobi!

BENSINGER. Hey, fellows. I'm trying to read.

WILSON. *(Also near window)* They're changing the guards down there. Look—they've got sixteen of them.

*(VOICES from the courtyard—"Hey!" "Hurry up." "Get a move on, Carl!")*

McCUE. *(Hands back contract)* You're going to miss a swell hanging, Hildy.

HILDY. I've seen better hangings than you'll ever hear of.

MURPHY. *(Turning to HILDY)* So you're going into the advertising business, eh? Writing poetry about Milady's drawers?

ENDICOTT. Are you going to wear an eye shade?

WILSON. I'll bet he has a desk with his name on it, and a stenographer.

MURPHY. You'll be like a firehorse tied to a milk wagon.

ENDICOTT. *(To MURPHY)* I don't know what gets into these birds. Can you imagine punching a clock, and sitting around talking like a lot of stuffed shirts about statistics?

HILDY. *(Crossing up Center)* Yah—sour grapes, that's all it is. Sour grapes.

MURPHY. I got a dumb brother went in for business. He's got seven kids and a mortgage, and belongs to a country club. He gets worse every year. Just a fathead.

HILDY. *(Putting on vest)* Listen to who's talking.

Journalists! Peeking through keyholes! Running after fire engines like a lot of coach dogs! Waking people up in the middle of the night to ask them what they think of campanionate marriage. Stealing pictures off old ladies of their daughters that get raped in Oak Park. A lot of lousy, daffy, buttinskis, swelling around with holes in their pants, borrowing nickels from office boys! And for what? So a million hired girls and motormen's wives'll know what's going on.

MURPHY. Your girl must have handed you that line.

HILDY. *(Putting on coat)* I don't need anybody to tell me about newspapers. I've been a newspaperman fifteen years. And if you want to know something, you'll all end up on the copy desk—gray-haired, humpbacked slobs, dodging garnishees when you're ninety. *(He crosses down Left.)*

SCHWARTZ. Yah, and what about you? How long do you think you'll last in that fancy job?

(HILDY *is unstrapping his suitcase.)*

ENDICOTT. You'll get canned cold the minute your contract's up, and then you'll be out in the street.

KRUGER. Sure—that's what always happens.

HILDY. Well, it don't happen to me. And I'll tell you why, if you want to know. Because my girl's uncle owns the business, that's why. *(He throws back the lid of the suitcase)* Now tie that.

WILSON. Has he got a lot of jack?

HILDY. It's choking him. You know what he sent us for a wedding present?

MURPHY. A dozen doilies.

HILDY. *(Crosses Center to table for parcel)* I wouldn't tell you bums, because it's up in high finance and you wouldn't understand it.

ENDICOTT. Probably gave you a lot of stock in the company, that you can't sell.

KRUGER. I know those uncles.

HILDY. *(Putting extra shirt in top of suitcase)* The hell he did! He gave us five hundred in cash, that's what he gave us.

McCUE. Go on!

SCHWARTZ. There *ain't* five hundred in cash.

HILDY. Yah? *(Pulling out a roll)* Well, there it is—most of it, except what it costs to get to New York.

McCUE. Jese, let's see.

HILDY. Oh, no!

MURPHY. How about a finif till tomorrow?

HILDY. I won't be here tomorrow. And that reminds me. *(Takes out a little book and crosses Center to MURPHY)* It comes to— *(Consults book)* Eight dollars and sixty-five cents altogether, Jimmy. Eight dollars and sixty-five cents.

(SCHWARTZ *rises and crosses Left slowly.*)

MURPHY. What does?

HILDY. That includes that four bucks in front of the Planters' Hotel when you were with that waitress from King's.

MURPHY. I thought I paid that.

HILDY. No. *(Reading from notes)* Herman Schlosser—altogether twenty dollars and—

McCUE. Ha! Ha! Ha!

ENDICOTT. Ho! Ho! Ho!

HILDY. All right. I guess I might as well call it off, all around. I should have known better than to try to collect, anyhow. *(Tears out the page and throws it at MURPHY)* You might say thanks. *(Crosses down Left to suitcase.)*

MURPHY. Not after that waitress.

SCHWARTZ. *(Leaning over to whisper to HILDY)* About that fifty bucks, Hildy. If you want a note—

HILDY. What fifty bucks? Aw, forget it.

SCHWARTZ. You see, it wasn't only the wife taking sick, (JENNIE, *the scrubwoman enters up Right. She receives an ovation. "Yea, Jennie!" "Jennie!" "Well, if it ain't Jennie," etc.)* but then besides that—

(JENNIE *puts down bucket and stands Center.* SCHWARTZ *crosses up Left to cooler.* HILDY *wheels, still kneeling.)*

KRUGER. I hear you just bought another apartment house, Jennie!

(JENNIE *laughs.)*

MURPHY. I hear you've fallen in love again, Jennie!
JENNIE. Can I wash up now, please?
BENSINGER. Yeah. This place smells like a monkey cage.
HILDY. *(Rising and crossing up Center to* JENNIE) Go on! You don't want to wash up on a night like this! This is a holiday! I'm going away, Jennie! Give us a kiss!
JENNIE *(Squealing)* Now you Hildy Johnson, you keep away from me! I'll hit you with this mop! I will. *(She brandishes the mop.)*
HILDY. What's the matter? Ain't I your fellow any more? I'll tell you what we'll do, Jennie! You and I'll go around and say goodbye! Everybody in the building!
McCUE. Hey, the Warden called you up! Wants to see you before you go!
HILDY. There you are, Jennie! We're invited! He invited Jennie, didn't he? (HILDY *crosses Right Center)* You bet he did!
JENNIE. Now you know he didn't.
HILDY. *(Lifting pail of water)* Only we can't carry a lot of water all over. *I* know! *(At window)* Hey! Jacobi! Look! *(Throws water out.)*

(JENNIE *giggles hysterically.)*

VOICE. *(Off)* Who did that?

SCHWARTZ. *(Crossing Right)* Cripes! Somebody's liable to come up.

HILDY. *(Crossing Center to* JENNIE) Come on, Jennie! We'll say goodbye to the Warden!

JENNIE. *(Struggling)* No, no! You let go of me! The Warden'll be mad! He'll do something.

HILDY. *(Grabbing her mop)* Never mind him! I own this building! Come on! *(In door up Right)* If my girl calls up, tell her I'm on my way!

*(He sings "Waltz Me Around Again, Jennie." Coy screams from* JENNIE, *as he waltzes her around holding mop behind her, and exits.)*

BENSINGER. Thank God that's over.

*(*ENDICOTT *sits in his chair.)*

KRUGER. What's the *Examiner* going to do with Hildy off the job?

WILSON. *(Sitting Right)* It must be great to walk into a place and quit.

McCUE. *(Sliding forward on table. In phone)* Yah. Diversey three two hundred.

ENDICOTT. I got an offer from the publicity department of the stockyards last year. I shoulda took it.

SCHWARTZ. What I'd like would be a job on the side.

McCUE. A desk and a stenographer. That wouldn't be so bad. I wouldn't mind a nice big blonde.

MURPHY. *(Graphically)* With a bozoom!

*(PHONE rings.)*

McCUE. *(At his own phone)* Hello, Sarge. McCue. Anything doing?

WILSON. *(Answering other phone)* Hello!—Press room?

McCUE. *(In phone)* Well, is the Sarge there?

WILSON. *(His tone becomes slightly formal)* Yes, Ma'am— No, Hildy ain't here just now, Madam. He left a message for you, though— Why, he said he was on his way— No, he didn't say where—just that he was on his way— All right, I'll tell him, Ma'am. *(Hangs up)* Oooh! Is she sore?

SCHWARTZ. *(Crossing Center to his chair)* Hildy oughtn't to do that. She's a swell kid.

McCUE. All right! Thank you, Sarge! *(Hangs up)* A hundred and fifty bucks a week! Can you imagine!

KRUGER. Probably gets Saturdays and Sundays off, too.

WILSON. And Christmas.

(MOLLIE *enters up Right.* MOLLIE MALLOY *is a North Clark Street tart.)*

McCUE. I wonder who Walter'll send over here, in Hildy's place.

MURPHY. Hello, Mollie!

ENDICOTT. Well, well! Here's the Moll.

WILSON. Hello, kid! How's the old liver?

McCUE. *(With bogus accent)* Shure, and how are yez, Mollie?

MOLLIE. *(Crossing down Center)* I've been looking for you bums.

MURPHY. Going to pay a call on Williams?

SCHWARTZ. He's just across the courtyard.

KRUGER. Better hurry up—he hasn't got all night.

McCUE. Yes, he has!

ENDICOTT. Say, Mollie, those were pretty roses you sent Earl. What do you want done with them tomorrow morning?

MOLLIE. *(Low and tense)* A lot of wise guys, ain't you? Well, you know what I think of you—all of you.

MURPHY. Now,—keep your pants on, Mollie.

MOLLIE. *(To MURPHY)* If you was worth breaking my fingernails on, I'd tear your puss wide open.

MURPHY. What you sore about, sweetheart? Wasn't that a swell story we give you?

MOLLIE. You cheap crumbs have been making a fool out of me long enough!

ENDICOTT. Now what kind of language is that?

BENSINGER. She oughtn't to be allowed in here!

MOLLIE. I never said I loved Earl Williams and was willing to marry him on the gallows! You made that up! And all that other bunk about my being his soulmate and having a love nest with him! *(She crosses up Center.)*

McCUE. Well, didn't you?

ENDICOTT. You've been sucking around that cuckoo ever since he's been in the death house. Everybody knows you're his affinity!

MOLLIE. *(Turns to* ENDICOTT*)* That's a lie! I met Mr. Williams just once in my life, when he was wandering around in the rain without his hat and coat on, like a sick dog. The day before the shooting. And I went up to him like any human being would, and I asked him what was the matter, and he told me about being fired after working at the same place twenty-two years and I brought him up to my rooms because it was warm there. *(She crosses Left Center.)*

ENDICOTT. Did he have the two dollars?

MURPHY. Aw, put it on a victrola record.

MOLLIE. Just because you want to fill your lying papers with a lot of dirty scandal, you got to crucify him and make a bum out of me!

ENDICOTT. Aw, go on!

MOLLIE. I tell you he just sat there talking to me— all night! He just sat there talking to me, and never once laid a hand on me, and in the morning he went away, and I never seen him again till the day of the trial.

ENDICOTT. Tell us what you told the jury!

*(The* REPORTERS *laugh.)*

MOLLIE. Go on, laugh! Damn you! Sure I was his

witness—the only one he had. Yes, me! Mollie Malloy! A Clark Street tart! I was the only one with guts enough to stand up for him! And that's why you're persecuting me!! Because he treated me decent, and not like an animal, and I said so!

ENDICOTT. Why didn't you adopt him instead of letting him run around shooting policemen?

SCHWARTZ Suppose that cop had been your own brother?

MOLLIE. I wish to God it had been one of you!

MURPHY. Say, what's the idea of this song and dance, anyhow! This is the press room. We're busy.

SCHWARTZ. Go on home.

MURPHY. Or go and see your boy friend.

McCUE. Yah—he's got a nice room.

ENDICOTT. He won't have it long. He's left a call for seven A.M.

MOLLIE. *(Crosses up Right Center before speaking)* It's a wonder a bolt of lightning don't come through the ceiling and strike you all *dead*!! *(She crosses Right to window. At the sound of the GALLOWS)* What's that? Oh, my God! *(Begins to cry, covering her face with her hands.)*

BENSINGER. *(Rising)* Say, what's the idea? *(To the* OTHERS) She oughtn't to be allowed in here.

MOLLIE. *(Taking cue "idea")* Talking that way about a fellow that's going to die.

ENDICOTT. Now don't get hysterical.

MOLLIE. *(Sobbing)* Shame on you! Shame on you!

SCHWARTZ. Come on, Mollie, go on home. Be a good girl.

MOLLIE. A poor little crazy fellow. Sitting there alone, with the Angel of Death beside him. *(She turns and takes a step Left)* And you cracking jokes.

MURPHY. *(Getting up meaningly)* Listen, if you don't shut up, I'll give you something good to cry about! *(He crosses and grabs* MOLLIE'S *arm.)*

MOLLIE. Keep your dirty hands off me!

MURPHY. *(He turns her around and pushes her to the door up Right)* Outside, bum!

MOLLIE. *(Going through the door)* You low down heels! You dirty punks! *(Exits.)*

MURPHY. *(Slams the door. A pause. He looks at hole in sleeve)* The nerve of that streetwalker.

McCUE. Whew!

MURPHY. *(Crosses down Center; gets coat)* You guys want to play some more poker?

ENDICOTT. *(Rising and crossing Right)* What's the use? I can't win a pot.

MURPHY. *(Crossing up Right)* Well, Jese, I'm a big loser.

WILSON. Me too. I must be out three dollars, anyhow.

ENDICOTT. *(Looking at* SCHWARTZ*)* It's damned funny who's got it.

SCHWARTZ. Don't look at me. I started with five bucks, and I got two-eighty left.

McCUE. *(Who has taken up the phone again)* Michigan eight thousand.

*(*SHERIFF HARTMAN *enters. He has come to raise hell, but an ovation checks him.* BENSINGER *puts down his book;* McCUE *abandons his telephoning.)*

KRUGER. Hello, Sheriff.

MURPHY. Well, if it ain't the old statesman himself. *(He ties his tie.)*

ENDICOTT. *(This speech coming out solo, after all the noise)* Got any news, Sheriff?

SHERIFF. *(Briefly)* Hello, fellas. *(He crosses down Center)* Now, who dumped that bucket of water out the window?

KRUGER. What bucket of water?

SHERIFF. Who threw it out the window is what I asked, and I want to know!

MURPHY. Judge Pam threw it out.

SHERIFF. I suppose Judge Pam threw that bottle!

ENDICOTT. Yeah. That was Judge Pam, too.

MURPHY. He was in here with his robes on, playing fireman.

SHERIFF. Come on now, fellows, I know how it was. *(Wheedingly)* It was Hildy Johnson, wasn't it? Where is he?

McCUE. *(Crossing Right)* Out with a lady! *(Sits in ENDICOTT's chair.)*

ENDICOTT. Hildy's quit, Sheriff. Didn't you hear?

SHERIFF. *(Crossing down Center)* Well, I'm glad of it. It's good riddance! Now personally, I don't give a God damn, but how do you suppose it looks to have a lot of hoodlums yelling and throwing things out of windows? *(In a subdued voice)* Besides, there's somebody *in* that death house. How do you suppose he feels, listening to all this re-vel-ery?

MURPHY. A hell of a lot you care how he feels!

SCHWARTZ. Keep your shirt on, Pinky.

SHERIFF. *(Crossing Right Center)* Wait a minute, you! I don't want to hear any more of that Pinky stuff. I got a name, see? Peter B. Hartman.

MURPHY. What's the matter with Pinky?

McCUE. *(Taking the cue)* He's all right.

MURPHY. Who's all right? }
ENDICOTT. Who's all right? } *(Together.)*

SHERIFF. Now stop! *(He paces up Center. Then turns)* Honest, boys, what's the idea of hanging a name like that on me? Pinky Hartman. How's that look to the voters? Like I had sore eyes or something.

MURPHY. You never heard of Bathhouse John kicking, did you?

WILSON. Or Hinky Dink?

ENDICOTT. It's made you famous!

SHERIFF. I swear I don't know what to do about you fellows. You abuse every privilege you get. I got a damn good notion to take this press room away from you.

MURPHY. That would be a break.

ENDICOTT. Yeah. The place is full of cockroaches anyway.

BENSINGER. *(Rises.* SHERIFF *comes to him)* Wait a minute, fellows— Now listen, Pete, this is the last favor I'm ever going to ask you, and it ain't me that's asking it. Get me? You know who's asking it— *(He takes off glasses)* a certain party is asking it. Once and for all, how about hanging this guy at five o'clock instead of seven? It ain't going to hurt you and we can make the City Edition.

SHERIFF. Aw, now, Roy, that's kind of raw. You can't hang a fella in his sleep, just to please a newspaper.

MURPHY. *(Crosses to Center)* No, but you can reprieve him twice so the hanging'll come three days before election. So you can run on a law and order ticket! You can do that all right! *(He picks up cigar from table and crosses up Right and sits in window.)*

SHERIFF. I had nothing whatsoever to do with those reprieves. That was entirely up to the Governor.

ENDICOTT. And who told the Governor what to do?

SCHWARTZ. How do we know there won't be another reprieve tonight? For all I know I'm hanging around here for nothing! When I've got a sick wife!

WILSON. Yah, with another alienist getting called in!

MURPHY. *(Taking cue "alienist")* This Wop or whatever he is!

SCHWARTZ. *(Rising and crossing Center)* Sure— what's all that about? Suppose he finds out he's insane or something?

SHERIFF. He *won't* find he's insane. Because he isn't. This ruse of reading the Declaration of Independence day and night is pure fake. But I've got to let this doctor see him, on account of his being sent by these Personal Liberty people, or whatever they call themselves. You and I know they're nothing but a bunch of Bolsheviks, but a hanging is a serious business. At a time like this you want to please everybody.

ENDICOTT. Everybody that can vote, anyhow.

SHERIFF. Now he's going to look him over in my office in a couple of minutes, and then you'll know all about it. Besides, there's nothing he *can* find out. Williams is as sane as I am.

SCHWARTZ. *(Crosses Right Center before speaking)* Saner! *(Sits in his chair.)*

SHERIFF. This hanging's going to come off exactly per schedule. And when I say "per schedule" that means seven o'clock and not a minute earlier. There's such a thing as being humane, you know.

BENSINGER. *(Turning away)* Just wait till *you* want a favor.

SHERIFF. *(Taking out tickets)* Now here are the tickets. Two for each paper.

*(McCUE crosses Center first. Then ENDICOTT, getting Left of SHERIFF. BENSINGER gets his and sits.)*

McCUE. What do you mean, two for each paper?

KRUGER. Hey, Mike!

SHERIFF. What do you want to do—take your family?

*(McCUE crosses up Center to his table.)*

SCHWARTZ. *(Crossing Center)* Now listen, Pinkie! I promised a pair to Ernie Byfield. He's never seen a hanging.

*(ENDICOTT hands ticket to KRUGER.)*

WILSON. *(Rising and crossing Center)* And the boss wants a couple for the advertising department.

SHERIFF. *(Giving out tickets)* This ain't the "Follies," you know. I'm tired of your editors using these tickets to get advertising accounts.

*(WILSON crosses Right, below table. MURPHY crosses Center.)*

ENDICOTT. You got a lot of nerve! Everybody knows what *you* use 'em for—to get in socially.

MURPHY. He had the whole Union League Club over here last time. (MURPHY *sits in his chair Center. Picks up funny paper.)*

ENDICOTT. Trying to suck in with Chatfield Taylor. I suppose you'll wear a monocle tomorrow morning.

SHERIFF. Now that ain't no way to talk, boys. If any of you want a couple of extra tickets, why I'll be more than glad to take care of you. Only for God's sake don't kill it.

SCHWARTZ. *(Taking tickets he crosses and sits in his chair)* Now you're talking.

WILSON. *(Crossing Right)* That's more like it. (WILSON *sits Right.)*

SHERIFF. Only you fellows got to lend a hand with us once in a while. We got a big job on our hands, smashing this Red menace—

ENDICOTT. We gave you four colums yesterday. What do you want?

SHERIFF. *(Turns to* ENDICOTT) That ain't it. The newspapers got to put their shoulders to the wheel. They've got to forcibly impress on the Bolsheviks that the death warrant for Earl Williams is a death warrant for the whole criminal element in this town. This hanging means more to the people of Chicago to-day— *(To* MURPHY, *who is reading a comic supplement)* this is a statement, Jimmie. What's the matter with you?

MURPHY. Aw, go home.

SHERIFF. All right, you'll just get scooped. Now we're going to reform these Reds with a rope. That's our slogan. *(To* ENDICOTT) Quote me if you want to. "Sheriff Hartman pledges that he is going to reform the Reds with a rope."

ENDICOTT. Oh, for God's sake, Pinky! We've been printing that chestnut for weeks! *(He exits Left into toilet.)*

SHERIFF. *(Moving Left after him)* Well, print it once more, as a favor to me.

WILSON. Anyhow you don't have to worry about the election. You're as good as in now, with the nigger vote coming around.

SHERIFF. *(Crossing up Center)* I was never prejudiced against the Negro race in any shape, manner, or form.

MURPHY. Are you still talking?

*(PHONE rings.)*

SHERIFF. During the race riots I just had to do my duty, that's all. And of course I was *misunderstood.*

KRUGER. Go on! You're a Southern gentleman, and you know it.

SHERIFF. *(Crossing Left)* Now boys!

MURPHY. *(In bogus Negro dialect)* Shush! Massa Hartman of the Vahginia Hartmans.

*(PHONE on small table rings. McCUE heads for it as SCHWARTZ answers.)*

SCHWARTZ. *(In phone)* Press room!

ENDICOTT. *(From toilet)* Hey, Pinky, I hear you used to own slaves.

SHERIFF. *(With a nervous laugh)* Now, fellows, this ain't the time to keep—

SCHWARTZ. Hey, he's here— For you, Sheriff.

SHERIFF. Me? *(He crosses up Center to phone)* Sheriff Hartman talking— *(A complete change of tone)* Oh, hello, dear.

KRUGER. *He's* hooked.

SHERIFF. Why, no, I didn't figure on coming home at all— Well, you see on account of the hanging being so early—

MURPHY. Tell her she's getting a break when you don't go home.

(ENDICOTT *enters Left with magazine.*)

SHERIFF. But you see this is business, dear. You don't think a hanging's any fun for me!

ENDICOTT. Music for this, Ernie!

SHERIFF. *(Agitatedly motions for silence)* But I have a whole lot to do first—getting things ready.

MURPHY. Why don't you take him out of your house and hang him?

SHERIFF. I'll call you up later, Irma— I'm not in my own office now. Besides. I've got to meet an alienist— No—alienist. Not me—Williams.

(HILDY *enters up Right, bringing back* JENNIE'S *mop. He throws it at* McCUE.)

HILDY. Boy, we cleaned up! (HILDY *crosses down Left to suitcase. He begins arranging things in the suitcase.*)

(ENDICOTT *crosses up Left, puts magazine on desk.*)

SHERIFF. I'll call you later, dear. *(Hangs up; crosses to* HILDY *down Left)* Now Johnson, what the hell do you mean? Throwing things out of windows. Who do you think you are?

HILDY. Who wants to know?

SHERIFF. You think you and Walter Burns are running this town! Well, I'm going to send a bill to the *Examiner* tomorrow for all the wreckage that's been committed around here in the past year! How do you like that?

HILDY. I think that's swell! You know what else you can do?

SHERIFF. *(Belligerently)* What?

HILDY. Guess.

SHERIFF. You stick your nose in this building tomorrow and I'll have you arrested!

HILDY. It's damn near worth staying for!

SHERIFF. And I'll tell you another thing, and you can pass it on to Walter Burns! The *Examiner* don't get any tickets for this hanging after the lies they been printing! You can make up your story like you do everything else out of whole cloth. (SHERIFF *crosses up Right to door.*)

HILDY. *(Rising and following* SHERIFF) Listen, you big pail of lard! If I wanted to go to your God damn hanging I'd go—see? And sit in a box!

SHERIFF. The hell you would!

HILDY. And I'd only have to tell *half* of what I know, at that!

SHERIFF. You don't know *anything*.

HILDY. *(Leaning against door)* No? Tell me, Mr. Hartmann, where'd you spend the night before the last hanging? At the Planters' Hotel with that librarian. Room Six Hundred and Two. And I got two bellboys and a night manager to prove it!

(HILDY *and* SHERIFF *shake their fingers at each other.*)

SHERIFF. If I didn't have to go and see that alienist I'd tell you a few things. (SHERIFF *exits.*)

HILDY. *(Calling after him)* And if I were you I'd get two tickets for the hanging over to Walter Burns pretty fast, or he's liable to come over here and stick a firecracker in your pants! *(Calmly to the* OTHERS. *He crosses down Left and arranges suitcase)* That Planters crack doubled him up.

KRUGER. *(Picking up banjo)* Is it on the level?

McCUE. *(Crossing Right Center)* Say, that's a good thing to know.

WILSON. Hey! Hildy! Your girl called up.

HILDY. My girl? When? What did she say? *(Rises, starts for telephone on* McCUE's *table.)*

WILSON. Just after you went out. (WOODENSHOES *enters with sandwiches and ketchup)* And if you'll take my advice, you'll call her back.

HILDY. *(Sitting on table)* Why didn't you tell me?
McCUE. *(Taking sandwiches from* WOODENSHOES)
Yes, sandwiches!

(ENDICOTT *and* BENSINGER *cross Right to big table.)*

HILDY. *(At phone)* Edgewater two-one-six-four.
Was she mad at me?

(WOODENSHOES *crosses down Right, puts ketchup
on table.)*

McCUE. Did you bring the ketchup?
BENSINGER. How about my plain lettuce?
ENDICOTT. A hamburger for me!
SCHWARTZ. I ordered one, didn't I?
KRUGER. You did not! This way, Woodenshoes!

*(They are taking their sandwiches from* WOODEN-
SHOES, ENDICOTT *throws one at* KRUGER, BEN-
SINGER *crosses Left to his desk.)*

HILDY. Hello. Peggy?—Hello, there!
McCUE. Attaboy! (McCUE *crosses up Center, sits
in chair by his table)* God, I'm starved.
HILDY. Why, darling, what's the matter?
BENSINGER. For God's sake, I said gluten bread!
HILDY. But listen, sweetheart—there isn't anything
to cry about.
MURPHY. The service is getting terrible around here.
HILDY. But listen, darling, I had business to attend
to. I'll tell you all about it the minute I see you— Aw,
darling, I just dropped in here for one second—be-
cause I *had* to. I couldn't go away without saying
goodbye to the fellows. *(To the* OTHERS) Will you
guys talk or something? *(Back to phone.)*
MURPHY. No, we won't!
HILDY. But listen, darling. Yes, I— Of course I

handed in my resignation— Yes, I've got a taxi waiting— Right outside.

WOODENSHOES. Go easy on that ketchup, I'm responsible for that.

HILDY. I've got them right in my pocket, honey— Three on the eleven-eighteen. I'm bringing 'em right out, mile a minute.

WOODENSHOES. She says you fellows have got to pay something soon.

HILDY. Aw, darling, if you talk like that I'm going to go right out and jump in the lake. I swear I will, because I can't stand it. Listen.

KRUGER. We're listening.

HILDY. *(Into phone)* Darling— I love you. *(Appropriate music by* KRUGER*)* I said— I love you.

*(MUSIC again.)*

SCHWARTZ. Aw, give him a break, Ernie.

*(*KRUGER *stops playing.)*

HILDY. *(Into phone)* That's more like it.

WOODENSHOES. Are you finished with this? *(Reaching for ketchup.)*

McCUE. *(With his mouth full)* Mm.

*(*WOODENSHOES *crosses up Center.)*

HILDY. *(Into phone)* Feel better now?—Well smile. And say something— That's the stuff. That's better— Are you all packed?—Oh, swell— I'll be *right there*.

WOODENSHOES. You fellas ought to pay her a little something on account. *(Exits up Right.)*

*(PHONE rings.)*

WILSON. *(Taking "Examiner" phone)* **Yah?**

HILDY. Listen, darling, will you wear that little blue straw hat?

WILSON. Wait a minute—I'll see.

HILDY. And are you happy now?—I bet you're not as happy as I am.

WILSON. *(At his phone)* Hold the line a minute.

HILDY. Oh, I'll bet you anything you want— All right— All right— I'm on my way— Not more than fifteen minutes. *Really* this time— Bye. *(Hangs up and crosses down Left.)*

WILSON. For God's sake, Hildy—here's Walter again! Tell him to give us a rest, will you?

(ENDICOTT *crosses up Center.*)

HILDY. *(Crossing Right to phone)* Oh— *(Into phone)* You're just making a God damn nuisance of yourself. What's the idea of calling me up all the time.

WALTER'S VOICE. I want you to come over for a second.

HILDY. No.

WALTER'S VOICE. Just a second.

HILDY. I'm through with newspapers. I don't give a God damn what you think of me. I'm leaving for New York tonight. Right now. This minute. *(Hangs up.)*

(HILDY *crosses up Center.* WILSON *changes practical and dummy phones.* HILDY *crosses Right, pulls out dummy phone, crosses Right and throws it out of upper window.)*

KRUGER. Wrong number. *(He puts down banjo.)*

McCUE. For God's sake, Hildy.

ENDICOTT. You'll get us in a hell of a jam.

McCUE. You better put out them lights.

(ENDICOTT *crosses up Center, puts out LIGHTS.)*

BENSINGER. Haven't you got any *sense?*

HILDY. *(Out the window)* Tell Pinky to put that among his souvenirs! It'll give him something more to squawk about— *(He crosses down Left and closes suitcase)* If that lunatic calls up again— (ENDICOTT *crosses down Right, puts cane in trouser leg)* tell him to put it in writing and mail it to Hildebrand Johnson, care of the Waterbury-Adams Corporation, Seven thirty-five Fifth Avenue, New York City—

MURPHY. Put it on the wall, Mike.

ENDICOTT. *(With a huge mouthful, crosses up Center)* Waterbury what?

McCUE. Adams.

HILDY. *(Showing gloves)* How do you like those onions? Marshall Field!

McCUE. Very individual.

HILDY. *(Crosses up Center with suitcase. Starts to look for cane)* Where's my cane?

ENDICOTT. What cane?

HILDY. Come now, fellows. That ain't funny, who's got my cane?

MURPHY. Can you describe this cane?

HILDY. Aw, for God's sake! Now listen, fellows—

*(ENDICOTT crosses down Center.)*

KRUGER. Are you sure you had it with you when you came into the room?

SCHWARTZ Was there any writing on it?

HILDY. *(Diving into BENSINGER's desk)* Come on. Cut out the clowning. Where is it?

BENSINGER. Keep out of my desk! Of all the God damn kindergartens!

HILDY. I only got fifteen minutes. Now, cut the kidding. *(He exits Left)* My God, you fellows have got a sense of humor!

MURPHY. Aw, give him his fairy wand!

ENDICOTT. *(Produces cane from trouser leg)* Here it is, Gladys.

HILDY. *(Entering Left)* You had me worried. *(Picks up his suitcase)* Well, goodbye, you lousy wage slaves! *(HILDY crosses up Left Center, puts on coat and hat)* When you're crawling up fire escapes, and getting kicked out of front doors, and eating Christmas dinner in a one-armed joint, don't forget your old pal, Hildy Johnson!

ENDICOTT. Goodbye Yonson.

McCUE. So long, Hildy.

MURPHY. Send us a postcard, you big stewbum.

KRUGER. When'll we see you again, Hildy?

HILDY. The next time you see me I'll be riding in a Rolls-Royce, giving out interviews on success. *(He picks up suitcase and crosses Center.)*

BENSINGER. Goodbye, Hildy.

WILSON. Goodbye.

SCHWARTZ. Take care of yourself.

HILDY. So long, fellows. *(He strikes a pose in the doorway, starts on a bit of verse)*
"And as the road beyond unfolds"—

*(There is a terrific fusillade of SHOTS from the courtyard, followed by YELLING and SIREN. For a tense second, EVERYONE is motionless.)*

VOICES. *(Off)* Get the riot guns! (EVERYONE *rushes to the window except* HILDY *and* KRUGER) Spread out, you guys! Carlson! Jacobi!

*(SHOTS. 1st WINDOW LIGHT out.)*

WILSON. There's a jail break!

*(KRUGER gets up. Crosses Center.)*

*(WARN Curtain.)*

MURPHY. *(At window, simultaneously)* Jacobi! What's the matter? What's happened?

VOICES. *(Off)* Watch the gate! He's probably trying the *gate!*

## *(SHOTS.)*

SCHWARTZ. *(Out the window)* Who got away? Who *was* it?
VOICE. *(Off— Outside)* *Earl Williams!* Earl Williams.

### *(Cut down SIREN.)*

**(ALL** *rush to phones.* MURPHY *and* WILSON *by big table.)*

WILSON *and* BENSINGER. Who? Who'd he say?

**(**KRUGER *down Left.* ENDICOTT *and* SCHWARTZ *up Center.* McCUE *to his table. GONG, SIREN full. SHOTS.)*

MURPHY *and* SCHWARTZ. Earl Williams! It was Earl Williams! He got away!
McCUE. Holy God! Gimme that telephone! *(He works hook frantically)* Hurry! Hurry up! Will you! This is important.
SCHWARTZ. Jeez, this is gonna make a bum out of the *Sheriff!*

**(**HILDY *stands paralyzed, his suitcase in his hand. SHOTS. 1st Window crash.)*

McCUE. *(Screaming)* Look out!

*(SHOTS. 2nd Window crash.)*

MURPHY. Where you shooting, you God damn fools!
SCHWARTZ. There's some phones in the State's Attorney's office!

KRUGER. Yeah!

*(SEARCHLIGHT down. There is a general panic at the door. ALL exit. The REPORTERS leave as if a bomb had broken in a trench. HILDY is left alone, still holding his suitcase. It falls. He rushes down Center and grabs "Examiner" phone. Throws hat away. SHOTS.)*

HILDY. Aah— *(He lets go of the chair and takes one of the telephones)* Examiner? Gimme Walter Burns! Quick. Hello, Walter! Hildy Johnson! Forget that! Earl Williams just lammed out of the County Jail! Yep— Yep— Yep—don't worry! I'm on the job!

*(There is a third volley. SHOTS. Searchlight up. SHOTS. 3rd Window crash. HILDY is removing his overcoat as)*

## THE CURTAIN FALLS

## ACT TWO

SCENE: *The Scene is the same as Act I, the time is about twenty minutes later.*

*The big papers have been removed, the glass cleaned up. The desk is closed.*

*LIGHTS full up.*

MURPHY'S *chair is struck.* WILSON'S *stool is under the table.* KRUGER'S *chair is pushed out on a rake.*

DISCOVERED: JENNIE, *the scrubwoman, is stage Center at rise, sweeping up broken glass and doing a little miscellaneous cleaning. After a second* WOODENSHOES *enters up Right and looks around.*

WOODENSHOES. Where are all the reporters? Out looking for him?

JENNIE. They broke all the windows. And pulled off a telephone. *(Points)* Ayyy, those newspaper fellows. They're worse'n anything.

WOODENSHOES. *(Crossing down Center)* There wasn't any excuse for his escaping. This sort of thing couldn't *ever happen,* if they listened to me.

JENNIE. Oooh, they'll catch him. Those big lights.

WOODENSHOES. What good will that do Society? The time to catch 'em is while they're little kids. That's the whole basis of my crime prevention theory. (EN-DICOTT, *businesslike, enters up Right and makes for a phone Center;* WOODENSHOES *watches him cross, paying no attention to* JENNIE) It's all going to be written up in the papers soon.

JENNIE. Ooooh, what they print in the papers. I never seen anything like it.

WOODENSHOES. *(Turning to* ENDICOTT*)* Has anything happened, Mr. Endicott?

ENDICOTT. Endicott calling. Gimme a rewrite man.

WOODENSHOES. *(Reaching into his pocket)* You know, this would be just the right time for you to print my theory of crime prevention. *(Pulls out a map of Chicago.)*

ENDICOTT. *(Into phone)* Well, hurry it up.

WOODENSHOES. *(Sinking)* Now here I got the city split up in districts. I get them marked in red.

ENDICOTT. What? For God's sake, can't you see I'm— *(Into phone)* Hello! Gill?

WOODENSHOES. *(Hurt)* But you been promising me you'd—

ENDICOTT. *(Snatches paper)* All right— I'll take it home and study it. Now stop annoying me— I got to work! I can't sit around listening to you! Get out of here and stop bothering me! *(Back to phone.* WOODENSHOES *backs up Center.* JENNIE *is by desk)* Ready, Gill?—Now, here's the situation so far. *(Starts arranging some notes.)*

WOODENSHOES. *(To* JENNIE*)* He's going to take it home and study it. *(He exits.)*

ENDICOTT. Right!—At seven minutes after nine, Williams was taken to the Sheriff's private office to be examined by this Professor Eglehofer, and a few minutes later he shot his way out— (JENNIE *crosses up Center)* No—nobody knows where he got the gun. Or if they do, they won't tell— Yeah— Yeah— He run up eight flights of stairs to the infirmary, and got out through the skylight. He must have slid down the rainpipe to the street— Yeah— No, I tell you nobody knows where he got it. (MURPHY *enters)* I got hold of Jacobi, but he won't talk.

MURPHY. *(Bumping into* JENNIE*)* Outside, Jennie! Outside! *(Crosses down Right.)*

ENDICOTT. *(In phone)* They're throwing a dragnet

around the whole North side. Watching the railroads and Red Headquarters. The Chief of Police has ordered out every copper on the force and says they'll get Williams before morning.

(JENNIE *crosses down Right below table.*)

MURPHY. *(In phone)* Hello, sweetheart. Give me the desk, will you?

ENDICOTT. *(After a final look at his notes)* The Crime Commission has offered a reward of ten thousand dollars for his capture— Yeah— *(He half rises)* I'm going to try to get hold of Eglehofer. He knows that's happened, if I can find him. Call you back. *(Hangs up and exits swiftly.)*

MURPHY. Jennie! Every time we turn our backs you start that God damn sweeping.

JENNIE. *(Picking up her dust-pan, she crosses Left)* All right. Only it's dirty. I get scolded.

MURPHY. *(Into phone)* Murphy talking— No clue yet as to Earl Williams' whereabouts. Here's a little feature, though— A tear bomb—tear bomb—criminals cry for it—

(SHERIFF HARTMAN *appears in the doorway. He has been running around, shouting a million orders, and playing tag with all the reporters in Chicago. He is in his shirt sleeves, and his diamond-studded badge of office is visible. He gives a suggestion of Hindenburg on the Seven Fronts.)*

MURPHY. Yeh! Tear bomb.    ⎫
SHERIFF. *(As he enters)* To hell with   ⎬ *(Together.)*
the Mayor! If he wants me he knows  ⎭
where I am.

MURPHY. *(Into phone)* Get this. A tear bomb went off unexpectedly in the hands of Sheriff Hartman's bombing squad.

SHERIFF. *(Crossing down Right Center to* MURPHY*)* **What went off?**

MURPHY. *(In phone)* The following Deputy Sheriffs were rushed to Passavant Hospital.

SHERIFF. A fine fair-weather friend you are!

(KRUGER *enters. Crosses down Right.*)

MURPHY. *(Remorselessly, into phone)* Philip Lustgarten—

SHERIFF. *( A step up stage)* After all I've done for you.

(JENNIE *picks up papers on* McCUE's *table.*)

MURPHY. Herman Waldstein—

SHERIFF. *(A step further up stage)* Putting stuff like that in the papers!

MURPHY. Sidney Matsburg.

SHERIFF. *(Exiting)* That's gratitude for you!

MURPHY. Henry Koogh—

JENNIE. *(Going toward door up Center)* Ain't that terrible?

MURPHY. Abe Lefkowitz—

JENNIE. All those fellows. *(Exits.)*

KRUGER. *(Into his phone)* Give me rewrite.

MURPHY. And William Gilhooly. Call you back. *(Hangs up and exits.)*

*(Together.)*

KRUGER. *(Into his phone)* Ready?—A man corresponding to Earl Williams' description was seen boarding a southbound Cottage Grove Avenue car at Austen Avenue by Motorman Julius L. Roosevelt. (McCUE *enters, goes to his phone)* Yeah—Roosevelt. I thought it would make a good feature on account of the name.

McCUE. *(In phone)* McCue talking. Give me the desk.

KRUGER. All right. I'll go after it. Call you back. *(He rises.)*

McCUE. *(In phone)* Hello! Emil?

KRUGER. Pick anything up? *(Crossing up Center. Exits.)*

McCUE. No, nothing important. *(In phone)* Oh, hello Emil! Ready?—sidelights on the man hunt— Mrs. Henrietta Schlogel, fifty-five scrublady, was shot in the left leg while scrubbing the eight floor of the Wrigley Building by one of Sheriff Hartman's Special Deputies.

HILDY. *(Enters. Crosses down Center. As he walks on)* There goes another scrub lady. *(Goes to phone, on big table, but starts arranging notes. Does not remove receiver as yet.)*

McCUE. No, just a flesh wound. They took her to Passavant Hospital. *(Hangs up, gets up and starts to cross Center)* Any dope on how he got out?

HILDY. No! From all I can get they were playing stoop tag.

McCUE. *(Ready to go out the door)* How about Jacobi? Did he say anything to you?

HILDY. Not a word. (McCUE *goes.* HILDY *quickly picks up his receiver)* Gimme Walter Burns. *(He gets up and closes the door carefully; comes back to his phone, juggles hook.)*

WALTER'S VOICE. Hello!

HILDY. Walter? Say, listen. I got the whole story from Jacobi and I got it exclusive.

WALTER'S VOICE. Scooped them again, eh?

HILDY. That's right. And it's a pip, only listen. It cost me two hundred and sixty bucks, see?

WALTER'S VOICE. Spit it out. What have you got?

HILDY. Just a minute— I'll give you the story. I'm telling you first I had to give him all the money I had on me and it wasn't exactly mine. Two hundred and sixty bucks and I want it back.

WALTER'S VOICE. Did you find out if the Reds were behind the escape or—

HILDY. *(Taking cue "Reds")* Did you hear what I said about the money?

WALTER'S VOICE. You'll get your God damn money.

HILDY. All right. Then here's the story. It's the jail

break of your dreams. Dr. Max J. Eglehofer, a profound thinker from Vienna, was giving Williams a final sanity test in the Sheriff's office, you know, sticking a lot of pins in him to get his reflexes, and then he decided to re-enact the crime exactly as it had taken place, so as to study Williams' powers of co-ordination.

WALTER'S VOICE. Take the mush out of your mouth —for God's sake what happened?

HILDY. Well, I'm coming to it, God damn it! Will you shut up? Of course he had to have a gun to re-enact with—and who do you suppose supplied it? Peter B. Hartman. B. for brains.

WALTER'S VOICE. What are you doing, kiddin'?

HILDY. I tell you I'm not kiddin'—Hartman gave his gun to the professor, the professor gave it to Earl, and Earl shot the professor right in the belly. *Earl shot*

WALTER'S VOICE. My God, that's wonderful!

HILDY. Ain't it perfect? If the Sheriff had unrolled a red carpet like at a Polish wedding and loaned Williams an umbrella it couldn't be more ideal.

WALTER'S VOICE. Is this Eglestein dead yet?

HILDY. Eglehofer? No! They spirited him away to Passavant Hospital.

WALTER'S VOICE. Anybody got it?

HILDY. No, we got it exclusive. Now listen, Walter— It cost me two hundred and sixty bucks, for this story, and I want it back— I had to give it to Jacobi before he'd cough up his guts— Two hundred and sixty dollars, the money I'm going to get married on— *money to get married on*

WALTER'S VOICE. That's great, Hildy! Fine work!—

HILDY. Never mind about the fine work— I want the money.

WALTER'S VOICE. All right—get back on the story.

HILDY. No! I tell you I'm not going to cover anything else— I'm going away— Listen. you lousy stiff— (PEGGY *enters with suitcase*) I did this just as a personal favor. I gave Jacobi every cent I got, and I want it back right away!

WALTER'S VOICE. All right—all right, I'll send it over—you lousy Shylock.

HILDY. When will you send it over?

*(PEGGY crosses down Center.)*

WALTER'S VOICE. Starting a boy right away.

HILDY. Well, see that you do or I can't get married.

WALTER'S VOICE. Fifteen minutes.

HILDY. All right, tell him to run. I'll be waiting right here in the press room. *(Hangs up. Sees PEGGY. Rises.)*

PEGGY. What was that—over the telephone?

HILDY. *(Taking her suitcase)* Nothing. I was just telling Walter Burns I was all through that's all. Hello, darling. *(He crosses up. Puts suitcase down.)*

PEGGY. Hildy, you haven't done something foolish with that money?

HILDY. *(Crossing down Center to PEGGY)* No! No!

PEGGY. You still *have* got the rest of it?

HILDY. Of course. Gee, darling, you don't think for a minute—

PEGGY. I think I'd better take care of it from now on!

HILDY. Now listen, darling. I can look after a couple of hundred dollars all right—

PEGGY. Hildy, if you've still got that money, I want you to give it to me!

HILDY. Now, sweetheart, it's going to be perfectly all right—

PEGGY. Then you haven't got it.

HILDY. Not this minute, I—

PEGGY. You did something with it?

HILDY. No, no. He's sending it right over—Walter, I mean. It'll be here any minute.

PEGGY. *(Crossing down Left)* Oh, Hildy!

HILDY. *(Following)* Listen, darling, I wouldn't have had this happen for the world. But it's going to be all right. *(Turns her around)* Now, here's what happened! I was just starting out to the house to get you when this guy Williams broke out of jail. You know, the fellow they were going to hang in the morning.

PEGGY. *(Dully)* Yes, I know.

HILDY. Aw, now, listen, sweetheart. I *had* to do what I did. And—and the same thing when it came to the money— (PEGGY *turns away*) Aw, Peggy! Now listen. I shouldn't tell you this, but do you know how this guy escaped? He was down in the Sheriff's office when Hartman—that's the Sheriff—and Eglehofer—that's this fellow from Vienna—

PEGGY. *(Crossing up to desk)* Hildy!

HILDY. Aw, now I can't tell you, if you won't listen. I had to give him the money so he wouldn't give the story to anybody else. Jacobi, I mean. That's the Assistant Warden. I got the story exclusive. *(Turns her around)* The biggest scoop in years, I'll bet.

PEGGY. Do you know how long Mother and i waited, out at the house?

HILDY. *(Taking her in his arms)* Aw, Peggy, listen. You ain't going to be mad at me for this. I couldn't help it. You'd have done the same thing yourself. I mean, the biggest story in the world busting, and nobody on the job.

PEGGY. *(Crossing down Center)* I might have known it would happen again.

HILDY. Aw, listen—

PEGGY. *(Turning on HILDY)* Every time I've ever wanted you for something—on my birthday and New Year's Eve, when I waited till five in the morning—

HILDY. But a big story broke!

PEGGY. It's always a big story—the biggest story in the world, and the next day everybody's forgotten it, even you!

HILDY. *(Coming towards her)* What do you mean forgotten? That was the Clara Hamon murder— I mean on your birthday. Peggy, it won't hurt you to wait five more minutes. The boy's on his way with the money now.

PEGGY. *(Facing him)* Mother's sitting downstairs waiting in a taxicab. I'm just ashamed to face her, the way you've been acting. If she knew about that money—it's all we've got in the world, Hildy. We haven't even got a place to sleep in, except the train and—

HILDY. Aw, gee, I wouldn't do anything in the world to hurt you, Peggy. *(He crosses to Left Center)* You make me feel like a criminal.

PEGGY. It's all that Walter Burns. Oh, I'll be so glad when I get you away from him. You simply can't resist him.

HILDY. *(Crossing Center to her)* Peggy, I've told you what I think of him. I wouldn't raise a finger if he was dying. *(Pointing to ground)* Honest to God!

PEGGY. Then why did you loan him the money?

HILDY. I didn't. You see, you won't listen to me, or you'd know I didn't. *(He turns way, then back suddenly)* Now, listen. I had to give the money to Jacobi, the Assistant—

(WOODENSHOES *ushers in* MRS. GRANT.)

WOODENSHOES. Here they are, ma'am.

(WOODENSHOES *exits immediately.* HILDY *crosses up and brings* MRS. GRANT *down Center.*)

HILDY. Oh, hello, Mrs. Grant—Mother. I was just explaining to Peggy.

PEGGY. Mother, I thought you were going to wait in the cab?

MRS. GRANT. Well, I just came up to tell you the meter's gone to two dollars.

HILDY. Yah, sure. But that's all right—

MRS. GRANT. I had a terrible time finding you. First I went into a room where a lot of policemen were playing cards.

HILDY. Yah—yah!

MRS. GRANT. Then I met that policeman and I asked him where Mr. Johnson's office was. (MRS. GRANT *looks around room.)*

PEGGY. Now, listen, Mother. I think you'd better go downstairs and we'll come as soon as we can.

MRS. GRANT. You've got a big room, haven't you? Where do you sit?

HILDY. Now, I tell you what you do. You and Peggy go on over to the station and get the baggage checked— now here's the tickets.

PEGGY. Now, Hildy—

HILDY. I'll be along in fifteen minutes, maybe sooner.

MRS. GRANT. How do you mean—that you aren't going?

HILDY. Of course I am. *(He crosses to* PEGGY) Now, I'll meet you at the Information Booth— *(He crosses up Center.)*

PEGGY. *(Taking* MRS. GRANT *up Center)* Come, Mother. Hildy has to wait here for a few minutes. It's something to do with the office—he's getting some money.

MRS. GRANT. *(Stops)* Money?

HILDY. *(Turning from suitcase)* Yah—ah—they're sending over—it's my salary. They're sending over my salary.

MRS. GRANT. Your salary? At this hour?

HILDY. *(Crossing down Left Center)* Yah. They were awful busy.

MRS. GRANT. Do you know what I'm beginning to think?

HILDY. *(Afraid she has guessed the truth. He turns suddenly)* What?

MRS. GRANT. *(Crossing to* HILDY) I think you must be a sort of irresponsible type, or you wouldn't do things this way.

*(*MCCUE *enters. Crosses to his phone, with side glances at the* OTHERS.)*

PEGGY. *(Crossing to* MRS. GRANT) Now you stop picking on my Hildy, Mother.

MRS. GRANT. *(Taking one "stop")* And here you are standing here with the train leaving any minute—

HILDY. Now, Mother, I never missed a train in my life. You run along with Peggy—

McCUE. *(In phone. Taking cue "Train in my life")* Hello. McCue talking.

PEGGY. *(Pulling* MRS. GRANT *up Center)* Come on, Mother! We're disturbing people.

HILDY. *(Crossing up Right Center to suitcase)* This is my girl, Mac, and her mother, Mr. McCue.

McCUE. *(Tipping his hat)* Pleased to meet you. *(Back to phone)* Here's a hell of a swell feature on the manhunt. *(To* MRS. GRANT) Excuse my French! *(Into phone)* Mrs. Phoebe De Wolfe, eighty-six-one and a half South State Street, colored, gave birth to a pickaninny in a patrol wagon.

HILDY. *(Exiting)* Listen, Mother. You better run along. I'll put my suitcase in the cab.

PEGGY. *(Following* HILDY) Come along, Mother!

McCUE. With Sheriff Hartman's Special Rifle Squad acting as midwives.

MRS. GRANT. Mercy!

McCUE. *(To* MRS. GRANT) You ought to have seen 'em, ma'am. Well, Phoebe was walking along the street when all of a sudden she began having labor pains! *(*HILDY *and* PEGGY *appear and drag* MRS. GRANT *off. In phone)* No! Labor pains! Didn't you ever have labor pains? Righto!! She was hollering for her husband, who's been missing for five months, when the police seen her. And Deputy Henry Shereson, who's a married man saw what her condition was. So he coaxed her into the patrol wagon, and they started a race with the stork for Passavant Hospital.

HILDY. *(Entering hurriedly)* If a boy comes here for me, hold him. I'll be right back! *(Exits.)*

McCUE. *(Waves at* HILDY) Listen—when the pickaninny was born the Rifle Squad examined him care-

fully, to see if it was Earl Williams, who they knew
was a-hiding somewhere. *(Laughs at his own joke)*
They named him Peter Hartman De Wolfe in honor
of the Sheriff, and they all chipped in a dollar a piece
on account of it being the first baby—*(The* MAYOR
*enters, very businesslike)* ever born in a manhunt.
Wait a minute—here's the Mayor, himself. Maybe
there's a statement.

MAYOR. *(Crossing down Right)* Don't pester me
now, please. I got a lot on my mind.

McCUE. *(Into phone)* The Mayor won't say anything. *(He hangs up.)*

MAYOR. Have you seen Sheriff Hartman?

(MURPHY *and* ENDICOTT *enter.)*

McCUE. *(Rising)* Been in and out all night, your
Honor—

MURPHY. *(Crossing down Right Center)* Now listen
your Honor. We've got to have a statement—

ENDICOTT. *(Crosssing Center)* We go to press in
twenty minutes.

(McCUE *moves down Left Center.)*

MAYOR. I can't help that, boys. I have nothing to
say—not at this time.

MURPHY. What do you mean "not at this time"?
Who do you think you are, Abraham Lincoln?

ENDICOTT. Come on, cut the statesman stuff! What
do you know about the escape? How'd he get out?

MURPHY. *(Taking cue "know about the escape")*
Where'd he get the gun?

MAYOR. Wait a minute, boys— Not so fast!

ENDICOTT. Well, give us a statement on the election,
then.

MURPHY. What effect's all this going to have on the
colored voters?

MAYOR. Not an iota. (ENDICOTT *crosses up Center.*) In what way can a misfortune of this sort influence the duty of every citizen, colored or otherwise?

MURPHY. Baloney.

ENDICOTT. *(Crossing down Center)* Listen here, Mayor. Is there a Red Menace or ain't there? And how did he get out of that rubber jail of yours?

MCCUE. Are you going to stand the gaff, Mayor? Or have you picked out somebody that's responsible?

MURPHY. *(Innocently)* Is there any truth in the report that you're on Stalin's pay roll?

ENDICOTT. Yah—the Senator claims you sleep in red underwear.

MAYOR. Never mind the jokes. Don't forget that I'm Mayor of this town. (SHERIFF *enters.*) And that the dignity of my office— Hello, Hartman. I've been looking for you—

(MCCUE *and* ENDICOTT *leap at* SHERIFF. *He crosses down Center, gets out pad and pencil.*)

ENDICOTT. What's the dope, Pinkie? How did he get out?

MCCUE. *(Taking cue "The dope, Pinkie")* What was he doing in your office?

MURPHY. What's this about somebody gettin' shot?

ENDICOTT. Where did he get the gun?

SHERIFF. Just a minute, fellas.

MURPHY. Cut the stallin'! Who engineered the getaway?

ENDICOTT. Was it the Reds?

SHERIFF. Just a minute, I tell you. We've got him located!

MURPHY. Who? Williams?

ENDICOTT. Where?!    } *(Together.)*

MCCUE. Where is he?

SHERIFF. Out to the place where he used to live— On Clark Street— Just got the tip.

ENDICOTT. Holy God!

(ENDICOTT *and* McCUE *go up Center.*)     *(Together.)*

McCUE. Why didn't you say so?

SHERIFF. The Rifle Squad is just going out.

(McCUE *exits.*)

ENDICOTT. Where are they?

SHERIFF. *(Crossing up Center)* Downstairs. All the boys are with them.

MURPHY. *(Starting out in a hurry)* For the love of Mike!

ENDICOTT. *(As he exits)* Hey, there, Charlie!

SHERIFF. *(Calling into the hallway)* Report to me, Charlie, the minute you get there! I'll be in the building. *(Comes busily down Left to desk.)*

MAYOR. *(Taking off hat, he crosses to* SHERIFF*)* Pete, I want to talk to you.

SHERIFF. I ain't got time, Fred— Honest. I'll see you later.

MAYOR. Pete, there's one thing I've got to know. Did you yourself actually give Williams that gun?

SHERIFF. The Professor asked me for it. I didn't know what he wanted it for. I thought it was something scientific.

MAYOR. I couldn't believe it. I can't believe it. Your own gun—loaded, too.

(KRUGER *enters, whistling.*)

SHERIFF. Now listen, Fred—

KRUGER. *(Heading for phone, down Left, salutes* MAYOR*)* Oh, hello, Your Honor. Any statement on the Red uprising tomorrow?

MAYOR. What Red uprising?

SHERIFF. There'll be no Red uprising.

KRUGER. The Senator claims the situation calls for the militia.

MAYOR. *(Crossing Center)* You can quote me as saying that anything the Senator says is a tissue of lies.

KRUGER. *(Into phone)* Kruger calling.

SHERIFF. Why aren't you with the Rifle Squad? They've just gone out.

KRUGER. We've got a man with them. *(Into phone)* Here's a red hot statement from the Senator. Ready? —He says the City Hall is another Augean stables— Augean!—Oh, for God's sake! *(Turns)* He don't know what Augean means.

MAYOR. The Senator doesn't know, either.

KRUGER. *(Into phone)* Well, take the rest, anyhow. The Senator claims that the Mayor and the Sheriff have shown themselves to be a couple of eight-year-olds playing with fire. (MAYOR *looks at* SHERIFF.) Then this is quote: "It is a lucky thing for the city that next Tuesday is Election Day, as the citizens will thus be saved the expense of impeaching the Mayor and the Sheriff." That's all—call you back. *(Hangs up. Starts to exit. Salutes* MAYOR) How are you, Mayor? *(Exits.)*

MAYOR. *(Crossing up Left to* SHERIFF) Pete! I've got a mighty unpleasant task to perform.

SHERIFF. *(Beside himself)* Now listen, Fred, you're just gonna get me rattled.

MAYOR. *(Continuing inexorably)* Two years ago we almost lost the colored vote on account of that coon story you told at the Dixie Marching Club— Mandy and the travelling salesman—

SHERIFF. Why harp on that *now?*

MAYOR. Now you come along with another one of your moron blunders—the worst of your whole career. *(Crosses down Center.)*

SHERIFF. *(Following down Center)* Listen, Fred. Stop worrying, will you? Just do me a favor and stop worrying! I'm doing everything on God's green earth! I've just sworn in four hundred deputies!

MAYOR. Four hundred?! Do you want to bankrupt this administration?

SHERIFF. But, Fred, I'm only paying them twelve dollars a night.

MAYOR. Twelve dollars! For those God damn uncles of yours?

SHERIFF. *(With dignity)* If you're talking about my brother-in-law, he's worked for the city fifteen years.

MAYOR. *(Bitterly)* I know. Getting up fake tag days! Pete, you're through.

SHERIFF. *(Dithery)* What do you mean—through?

MAYOR. I mean I'm scratching your name off the ticket Tuesday and running Czernecki in your place. *(SHERIFF is thunderstruck as MAYOR continues)* It's nothing personal, Pete—it's the only way out— It's a sacrifice we all ought to be happy to make.

SHERIFF. *(As David to Jonathan)* Fred!

MAYOR. Now Pete! *(Holds up hand, and crosses down Left)* Please don't appeal to my sentimental side—

SHERIFF. *(Crossing down Center)* Fred, I don't know what to say. A thing like this almost destroys a man's faith in human nature—

MAYOR. I wish you wouldn't talk like that, Pete—

SHERIFF. Our families, Fred. I've always looked on Bessie as my own sister.

MAYOR. *(Wavering and desperate)* If there was any way out—

*(PHONE rings.)*

SHERIFF. There *is* a *way out*. I've got this Williams surrounded, haven't I? What more do you want? Now if you just give me a couple of hours— *(Into phone)* Hello! Hello! Hello! *(The PHONE keeps on. He sees it is the wrong one. He gets another)* Hello! *(He jumps up)* Four hundred suppers! Nothing doing! This is a manhunt—not a banquet—! The twelve dollars includes everything—! Well, the hell with them!

Earl Williams ain't eating, is he?! *(He hangs up and crosses Center)* That gives you an idea of what I'm up against!

MAYOR. *(Crossing Center to* SHERIFF*)* We're up against a lot more than that with that nutty slogan you invented. "Reform the Reds with a rope." (SHERIFF *winces)* Now, there ain't any God damn Reds, and you know it.

SHERIFF. Yah, but why go into that now, Fred?

MAYOR. Well, the slogan I had was all we needed to win— "Keep King George out of Chicago!"

SHERIFF. *(Crosses down Right)* I ain't had a bite to eat since this thing happened.

MAYOR. *(Following)* Pete, two hundred thousand colored votes are at stake! And we've got to hang Earl Williams to get them.

SHERIFF. But we're going to hang him, Fred. He can't get away.

*(A KNOCK on the door.)*

MAYOR. What do you mean he can't get away! He got away, didn't he? Now look here, Pete— *(KNOCKING louder.)* Oh, who's out there?

PINCUS. *(Outside)* Is Sheriff Hartman in there?

SHERIFF. *(Starts for door, relieved)* Ah! It's for me! *(Opens the door. A small man named* PINCUS *stands there)* I'm Sheriff Hartman. Do you want me?

(PINCUS *enters.* MAYOR *crosses Right.)*

PINCUS. Yes, *sir.* I've been looking all over for you, Sheriff. You're certainly a hard fellow to find.

MAYOR. *(Annoyed)* What do you want?

PINCUS. *(Taking a document from his pocket and proffering it to the* SHERIFF. *Smiles pleasantly)* From the Governor.

MAYOR. *(A step up stage)* What's from the Governor?

SHERIFF. Huh?

PINCUS. The reprieve for Earl Williams.

SHERIFF. *(Stunned)* For *who?*

PINCUS. *(Amiably)* Earl Williams. The reprieve. *(A ghastly pause—he takes off his hat)* I thought I'd never find you. First I had an awful time getting a taxi—

MAYOR. Wait—a minute. *(Getting his bearings. Crosses up Center)* Is this a joke or something?

PINCUS. Huh?

SHERIFF. *(He throws envelope away, and crosses down Left with reprieve)* It's a mistake—there must be a mistake! The Governor gave me his word of honor he wouldn't interfere! Two days ago!

MAYOR. *(Following)* And you fell for it! Holy God, Pete! *(PINCUS puts on hat and starts to go.)* It frightens me what I'd like to do to you! *(Turns to PINCUS)* Wait a minute! Come here you! Who else knows about this?

PINCUS. *(Crossing down Center)* They were all standing around when he wrote it. It was after they got back from fishing.

MAYOR. *(To SHERIFF)* Get the Governor on the phone, Hartman!

PINCUS. *(Pleasantly)* They ain't got a phone. They're duck-shooting now.

MAYOR. A lot of God damn Nimrods.

SHERIFF. *(Who has been reading the reprieve)* Can you beat that? Read it! *(Thrusts the paper into MAYOR's hands)* Insane, he says! *(Striding over to PINCUS. MAYOR crosses down Left reading)* He knows damn well Earl Williams ain't insane!

PINCUS. Yeah! But I—haven't got—

SHERIFF. This reprieve is pure politics and you know it! It's an attempt to ruin us!

MAYOR. Dementia praecox! My God!

SHERIFF. *(Crossing down Left)* We got to think fast before those lying reporters get hold of this. What'll we tell them?

*[handwritten margin note: Not honest]*

MAYOR. What'll we tell 'em? You can tell 'em your God damn relatives are out there shooting everybody they see, for the *hell of it!*

SHERIFF. Now, Fred, you're just excited. *(PHONE rings.* SHERIFF *starts up to* McCUE's *table for the phone, talking as he goes)* We aren't going to get any place, rowing like this.

MAYOR. *(Following up Left Center)* And you can tell 'em the Republican Party is through in this state on account of *you.*

SHERIFF. *(Gesturing)* Sssh. Wait, Fred. *(Excitedly, into phone)* What? Where?—Where? My *God!*

MAYOR. *(A quick whisper)* What is it?

SHERIFF. They got him! *(Back to phone)* Wait a minute—hold the wire. *(To the* MAYOR *again)* They got Earl Williams surrounded—the Rifle Squad had—in his house—

MAYOR. *(Looking at* PINCUS) Tell 'em to hold the wire.

SHERIFF. I did. *(Into phone)* Hold the wire.

MAYOR. Cover up that transmitter! (SHERIFF *does so.* MAYOR *looks at* PINCUS *and crosses to door and closes it.* PINCUS *follows him with his eyes.* MAYOR *crosses Center)* Now listen! You never arrived here with this—whatever it is. Get that?

PINCUS. Yes, I did!

MAYOR. Wait a minute! How much do you make a week?

PINCUS. Huh?

MAYOR. *(Impatiently)* How much do you make a week? What's your salary?

PINCUS. Oh! Forty dollars.

SHERIFF. *(Into phone)* No—don't cut me off.

MAYOR. How would you like to have a job for three hundred and fifty dollars a month? That's almost a hundred dollars a week?

PINCUS. Who? Me?

MAYOR. Who the hell do you think? (PINCUS *is a little startled; the* MAYOR *hastens to adopt a milder manner)* Now listen. There's a fine opening for a fellow like you in the City Sealer's office.

PINCUS. The what?

MAYOR. The City Sealer's Office.

PINCUS. You mean here in Chicago?

MAYOR. *(Impatient)* Yes, yes.

SHERIFF. *(Into phone)* Well, wait a minute, will you? I'm in conference.

PINCUS. No, I couldn't do that.

MAYOR. Why not?

PINCUS. I couldn't work in Chicago. You see, I've got my family in Springfield.

MAYOR. *(Desperate)* But you could bring 'em to Chicago! We'll pay all your expenses.

PINCUS. *(Maddeningly slow)* No, I don't think so.

MAYOR. Why not?

PINCUS. I got two kids going to high school there, and if I change them from one town to another they'd probably lose a grade.

MAYOR. No, they wouldn't—they'd gain one. They could go into any class they want to. And I guarantee that they'll graduate with highest honors!

PINCUS. *(Beginning to be interested)* Yah?

MAYOR. Now what do you say?

PINCUS. What did you say this job was?

MAYOR. In the City Sealer's office.

PINCUS. What's he do?

(MAYOR *crosses down Center.)*

SHERIFF. He has charge of all the important documents. He puts the City seals on them.

MAYOR. *(Crossing back to PINCUS)* That's about on a par with the rest of your knowledge. The City Sealer's duty is to see that the people of Chicago are not victimized by unscrupulous butchers and grocers.

SHERIFF. That's what I meant.

MAYOR. It's his duty to go around and test their scales.

PINCUS. Yeah?

MAYOR. But only twice a year.

PINCUS. *(Taking off hat)* Well, I don't know! This puts me in a hell of a hole.

MAYOR. No, it doesn't— *(Hands him reprieve)* Now remember. You never arrived here with this thing. You got caught in the traffic or something. Now get out of here. And don't let anybody see you— (MAYOR *goes up Center knocking* PINCUS'S *hat out of his hand.)*

PINCUS. *(Picking up hat)* But how do I know—

MAYOR. *(Unlocking door)* Come in and see me in my office tomorrow. What's your name?

PINCUS. Pincus.

MAYOR. All right, Mr. Pincus, all you've got to do is lay low and keep your mouth shut. Here! *(He hands him a card)* Go to this address. It's a nice homey little place, and you can get anything you want. *(He sees* PINCUS *through the door.)*

SHERIFF. *(On phone, pretty desperately by this time)* Hold your horses, for God's sake! I'll tell you in a minute!

MAYOR. *(Calling after* PINCUS*)* Just tell 'em Fred sent you! (MAYOR *locks door, and crosses up Center beside* SHERIFF*)* All right. Tell 'em to shoot to kill.

SHERIFF. What?

MAYOR. Shoot to kill, I said.

SHERIFF. I don't know, Fred. There's that reprieve if they ever find out.

MAYOR. Nobody reprieved that policeman he murdered. Now do as I tell you.

SHERIFF. *(Into phone)* Hello, Mittelbaum— Listen. *(His voice is weak. He looks at* MAYOR. *The* MAYOR *nods)* Shoot to kill— That's the orders—pass the word along.—No! We don't want him! And listen, Mittelbaum—five hundred bucks for the guy that does the job— Yes, I'll be right out there. *(Hangs up and crosses down Center)* Well, I hope that's the right thing to do.

*(There is a great KICKING on the door.)*

HILDY. *(Heard off)* Hey! Who's in there? Open that door!

MAYOR. *(Picking up hat)* Take the guilty look off your face. You're trembling like a horse.

*(The MAYOR starts up Center. The SHERIFF starts whistling "Ach, Du Lieber, Augustine," in what he imagines in a care-free manner. The MAYOR opens the door, HILDY enters.)*

HILDY. Oh, it's you two?

SHERIFF. *(With elaborate unconcern, as he walks toward the door)* Oh, hello, Hildy.

HILDY. Well, what's the idea of locking the door? Playing post office? *(Crosses down Center, sits, picks up phone.)*

MAYOR. Come on, Hartman! *(Exits.)*

HILDY. *(Into phone)* Gimme Walter Burns. *(To the OTHERS)* Was there a feller in here asking for me?

SHERIFF. *(In doorway)* Did you hear we've got Williams surrounded?

HILDY. Yah. I heard you only let him out so he could vote for you on Tuesday.

MAYOR. *(Off)* Hartman!

**(SHERIFF** *exits.)*

HILDY. *(Into phone)* Hello, Duffy—this is Hildy. Lis'sen, where's Walter? Well, where did he go? Duffy, I'm waitin' here for the boy to bring over my money—the two hundred and sixty dollars he owes me— Yeah—in the press room. He told me the boy was on his way— What the hell are you laughing about— Lis'sen, Duffy, has that maniac started the money over or not?— (WOODENSHOES *enters.)* No, I ain't got time to come over to the office. I'll miss the train— Oh—that double-crossing louse! *(He hangs up.)*

WOODENSHOES. *(Crossing down Center)* The trouble is, Mr. Johnson, nobody's using the right psychology. Now you take this aspect of the situation: you got a man named Earl Williams who has escaped—

HILDY. Have you got two hundred and sixty dollars on you?

WOODENSHOES. What?

HILDY. Have you got two hundred and sixty dollars?

WOODENSHOES. No, but—(HILDY *rises and crosses down Left)* I know how we can get ten thousand dollars, if you'll just listen. *(Pointing finger at* HILDY *in the manner of a man letting the cat out of the bag)* Serchay la femme!

HILDY. *What?*

WOODENSHOES. *(Inexorably, for him)* Who is it that's been defendin' this feller Williams right along? Who is it that was hangin' around his room just before the escape happened?

HILDY. *(Pacing)* Oh, I ain't got time, Woodenshoes. I got to get two hundred and sixty dollars in the next five minutes.

WOODENSHOES. It's gonna take longer than five minutes. I know where Earl Williams is.

HILDY. *(Crossing down Right)* He's out at Clark and Fullerton, getting his head blown off. But that don't get me any money.

WOODENSHOES. *(To* HILDY) Earl Williams is with that girl, Mollie Malloy! *That's* where he is!

HILDY. *(Crossing up Right)* Can you imagine— (LOUIE *enters.)* this time tomorrow I'd have been a gentleman.

LOUIE. *(Crossing down Center to* HILDY) Oh, here you are!

HILDY. *(Springing toward him)* Thank God! Have you got the dough?

(WOODENSHOES *backs up Center.)*

LOUIE. Huh?

WOODENSHOES. She sent him a lot of roses, didn't she?

HILDY. Never mind your roses— Come on, Louie! Gimme the dough! I'm in a hell of a hurry!

LOUIE. What are you talking about?

WOODENSHOES. And I'll betcha I'm right. *(He exits.)*

HILDY. Listen, Louie! Do you mean to say Walter didn't give you the dough he owes me? *(Together.)*

LOUIE. *(Trying to drag* HILDY *away)* Walter's pretty sore! You better come over and see him.

HILDY. But that's all settled, Louie. Everything's all right!

LOUIE. *(Weakening)* God, Hildy, I don't know.

HILDY. He *wants* me to go! Now, listen, Louie— you've always got a lot of money—will you help me out? This two hundred and sixty bucks— Walter's sending a boy with it, but I can't wait. I gotta catch a train, see? Now—

LOUIE. What two hundred and sixty bucks?

HILDY. The money I spent on the story! He's sending it over, but I want *you* to take *that* and give *me* the money *now!*

LOUIE. *(Finally getting it)* Oh! You want two hundred and sixty dollars—from me—now!

HILDY. *Yes!*

LOUIE. Well, that's a lot of money, you know what I mean?

HILDY. You can get it from Walter. I'll give you my I.O.U.

LOUIE. Lis'sen, Hildy, I'd like to help you out. But I've been stung on so many I.O.U's lately that I made myself a promise.

HILDY. *(Taking cue "many I.O.U's lately")* But this ain't an I-O-U— It's money comin' to me from the paper.

LOUIE. What have you got to show for it?

HILDY. *(Seizing* LOUIE's *arm tensely)* Louie, lis'sen!

My whole future is dependent on this. My girl's waitin' at the train. I've just got fifteen minutes to get there. If you'll help me out, I swear— Honest to God—

LOUIE. *(Taking cue, "me out, I swear—")* Two hundred and sixty dollars—that's a big gamble!

HILDY. *(Giving his "victim" the bum's rush)* It's no gamble at all! I'll write out a note to Walter sayin' for him to give you the money he owes me.

LOUIE. *(Crossing down Center)* Well, I'll tell you what I'll do with you. I'll take a chance.

HILDY. *(Crossing Center. Sits, starts to write)* That's the stuff. You're a white man, Louie, you're a real white man. God— I knew I could depend on you.

LOUIE. *(Counting roll)* I tell you what I'll do. I'll give you a hundred and fifty dollars for the debt.

HILDY. *(Stares at him)* That's taking advantage, Louie.

LOUIE. That's the best I can do.

HILDY. Why! I lose almost a hundred bucks by that.

LOUIE. All right. *(Starts to put money back in his pocket)* Have it your own way!

HILDY. *(Rises, crosses to* LOUIE, *grabs his arm)* Make it two hundred!

LOUIE. One hundred and fifty! *(Pause.)*

HILDY. All right, give me the dough.

LOUIE. *(Takes the paper that* HILDY *has written out and reads it very carefully, folds it, puts it in his pocket)* Here you are. *(*HILDY *grabs the money and begins to count it.* LOUIE *crosses up Center)* Well, goodbye, and good luck. I'll look you up in New York, if there's anything wrong with this. *(*LOUIE *exits.)*

HILDY. *(Counting the money)* Ten, twenty-thirty, thirty-five, forty-five—damn it! *(Gets confused. Starts again)* Ten, twenty, thirty, forty, forty-five—fifty-five— *(In trouble again, he gives up, he crosses up and starts to put on coat)* Oh, the hell with it. Anyway, I get out of this lousy place. *(He is arrested by a SOUND at the window down Right; the sound is caused by* EARL WILLIAMS *falling through the window into the room.* MR. WILLIAMS *is a little harmless looking man. He is coatless and is shod with death-house sneakers. He carries a large gun. He is on the verge of collapse and holds on to a chair for support. He talks in an exhausted voice.* HILDY *at the sight of him, throws the coat back on* McCUE's *table, and stands riveted)* They can take their story now and—

EARL. *(Crossing to chair at Right end of table)* They're after me with searchlights.

HILDY. Put—put down that gun!

EARL. *(Supporting himself on chair)* It ain't loaded. I fired all the bullets already.

HILDY. *(Crossing to door)* Holy God Almighty— *(He locks door.)*

EARL. *(Weakly)* I surrender— I couldn't hang off that roof any longer.

HILDY. Holy God! *(He crosses down Right. Shoves* WILLIAMS *away from window to position below table)* Get away from that window. *(He takes the gun away and puts it in hip pocket. He crosses up Right to light switch. Blackout.)*

EARL. I'm not afraid to die. *(*HILDY *crosses down Right, pulls shades.)* I was tellin' the fella that when he handed me the gun.

HILDY. Shut up a second!

EARL. *(Babbling on)* Wakin' me up in the middle of the night—stickin' pins in me—callin' me a Bolshevik—I'm not a Bolshevk— I'm an Anarchist!

HILDY. *(Crosses to* WILLIAMS, *looks at him, then looks for place to hide him)* Be quiet. The hell with that. Shut up—will you?

EARL. Go on— Take me back and hang me— I done my best. *(He crumples.)*

*(*HILDY *picks him up, carries him to door Left dumps him inside, leaves gun, crosses Right hurriedly, to "Examiner" phone.)*

HILDY. Hello. Gimme Walter Burns. *Quick!* (HILDY *grabs other PHONE which rings)* Hello. Hello. Oh, hello Peggy. Listen for God's sake, have a heart, will you? Something terrific has happened. *(Into "Examiner" phone)* Walter? Hildy.

WALTER'S VOICE. Sending the boy right away. Keep your shirt on.

HILDY. The hell with that. Listen—come right over here! Come over right away. Wait a minute.

WALTER'S VOICE. What the hell's the matter with you now—?

HILDY. *(Into other phone)* Peggy, quit bawling me out, will you? I'm in a hell of a jam—

WALTER'S VOICE. Hurry up.

HILDY. Walter. Get this. I only want to say it once. I got Earl Williams!

WALTER'S VOICE. What! You've caught him?

HILDY. Yes.

WALTER'S VOICE. Jesus H. Sebastian God—where?

HILDY. Here in the press room.

WALTER'S VOICE. You're a God damn liar—

HILDY. Honest to God!

WALTER'S VOICE. Got him stuck away?

HILDY. Yep. But for God's sake, hurry. I need you.

WALTER'S VOICE. Keep him sewed up for ten minutes.

HILDY. I will. *(Hangs up "Examiner" phone. Goes to other phone)* Listen, darling, this is the biggest thing that ever happened— Now, wait! Don't cry. Wait till I tell you. *(Lowers his voice)* I just captured Earl Williams. *(In an intense whisper)* Earl Williams!— the murderer! I got him—don't tell anybody— Aw, Peggy, Peggy— I can't—I can't now! Good Lord! Don't you realize— (MOLLIE *rattles door knob.) I know,* but Peggy— *(Apparently she has hung up)* Hello, Peggy—Peggy! (HILDY *bangs up the phone dejectedly. During the last few speeches, there has been a KNOCKING on the door.* HILDY *glares apprehen-*

*sively and holds himself ready for fight. He moves to the door, and as he approaches it, cries)* Who is it? *(There is no answer.* HILDY *opens the door, cautiously.* MOLLIE *bounds in. He shuts door, seizes her and wrestles with her)* Wait a minute, I tell you! What do *you* want?

MOLLIE. *(Grabbing him)* Where they gone? You know where they are.

HILDY. Get outa here, Mollie!

MOLLIE. *(Persistent)* They got him surrounded. They're gonna shoot him—like a dog.

HILDY. Listen! They're lookin' for you, too! If you're smart, you'll get outa here.

MOLLIE. For God's sake, tell me where they've gone? I ain't afraid of them, the yella murderers—

HILDY. I'll tell you where they are. They're out at Clark Street! That's where they are! Clark and Fullerton! *(He starts to open door.)*

MOLLIE. *(Taking cue, "Clark Street")* Where? Where? Where?

*(The door opens and* EARL WILLIAMS *appears Left and leans on* KRUGER'S *chair Left, dazed and blinking.* MOLLIE *sees him.)*

MOLLIE. Ohhhhhhhhhhhhhh!— *(She crosses down Center.)*

HILDY. *(Crossing down Left)* Oh, for—! *(A KNOCK.* HILDY *stops)* Who is it?

WOODENSHOES. *(Off)* It's me.

HILDY. What do you want, Woodenshoes?

WOODENSHOES. *(Still outside)* I got some important information for you—a clue—

HILDY. I'll be right with you. I'm makin' a personal call— *(To* MOLLIE, *in a tense whisper)* Get him back in there! *(Indicating door Left.)*

MOLLIE. *(Crossing Left to* HILDY*)* What's this—a double-cross?

HILDY. God damn it! I'm tryin' to save him—
WOODENSHOES. *(Outside)* This is very important.

(HILDY *starts to cross up Center.*)

MOLLIE. *(To* EARL) My God! How did you get here?

HILDY. *(Turning to* MOLLIE) Keep him *quiet!* It's a cop! *(Turning on his way to the door)* I'll get rid of him—

EARL. Thank you for those roses!

MOLLIE. *(Crossing Left)* Ssh!

(HILDY *opens the door wide, revealing* WOODENSHOES, *and steps quickly into the hall.*)

HILDY. Hello, Woodenshoes! What's on your mind?

WOODENSHOES. I'll tell you. I found a fellow who says—

MOLLIE. *(In a whisper)* How did you get here? Does anybody know? *(The door closes.)*

*(Together.)*

EARL. I came down the rainpipe. I didn't mean to shoot him. I don't know what happened.

MOLLIE. But what are you going to do? You can't stay here! They'll get you!

EARL. I don't care anymore.

MOLLIE. You've got to hide! You've got to hide somewhere!

EARL. No! I don't care. It's better to die for a cause than the way most people die.

MOLLIE. You won't die. They'll never get you.

EARL. I ain't important. It's humanity that's important, like I told you. Humanity is a wonderful thing, Mollie.

MOLLIE. No, it ain't. They're just dirty murderers. Look what they done to you—and me—

EARL. That's because they don't know any better.

MOLLIE. You're too good for 'em—that's why.

EARL. You're good, too.

MOLLIE. *(With wonder)* Me?

EARL. Yeah, I think you're wonderful— I wrote out a statement today. There was a lot about you in it. I said you were the most beautiful character I ever met.

MOLLIE. *(Blinking and dazed)* Yeah?

HILDY. *(Coming back, locks door and crosses down Left)* Better get back in there! The fellers are coming down the hall now!

MOLLIE. They'll find him there!

HILDY. Well, there isn't any place *else*.

*(He looks helplessly around the room; at that moment someone tries the DOOR KNOB.)*

MOLLIE. There's somebody!

HILDY. *(Turns, desperately)* Sssh!

ENDICOTT. *(Off)* Who locked the door!—

HILDY. Coming right away, Mike. *(He crosses Center)* He's got to go in there!

ENDICOTT. *(Off)* Well, hurry it up!

*(HILDY turns, sees desk.)*

MOLLIE. Oh, my God!

HILDY. Wait a minute! I've got an idea! *(Springs and throws swivel chair down stage—opens desk.)*

MOLLIE. *(Crossing up Left beside desk)* That's it!

HILDY. *(Crossing down, drags EARL to desk)* Can you get in this desk?

WILSON. *(Off)* What's going on in there? *(Starts to pound on door.)*

EARL. What good'll it do?

HILDY. *(Shoves him in desk)* We'll get you out in ten minutes.

*(POUNDING on the door.)*

WILSON. *(Off) Open up* there, will you?
HILDY. All right, all right, all right.
MOLLIE. *(To* EARL) Go on! Please! Please!
EARL. *(In the process)* They'll find me, *anyhow.*
*(More POUNDING.)*

HILDY. All right, I'm coming! *(To* EARL *as he closes lid)* Now keep dead quiet! Don't even breathe! *(He crosses up Center.)*
MOLLIE. I'll be right here. I won't leave you. (MOLLIE *grabs swivel chair, wheels it in front of desk, and sits. She starts to powder her nose.)*
ENDICOTT. *(Off)* Hey, what the hell!
HILDY. Keep your shirt on! Hey! *(He opens the door)* What are you trying to do! Kick down the building?

(ENDICOTT *and* WILSON *enter.* ENDICOTT *crosses up Center as* HILDY *backs away.* WILSON *crosses down Right to phone at end of table. Sits.)*

WILSON. *(As he enters)* Well, for God's sake!
ENDICOTT. Kind of exclusive, ain't you? *(Sees* MOLLIE) Oh! *(Elaborately)* I beg your pardon.
WILSON. City desk, please! What's the idea of locking the door?
HILDY. *(Backing against desk)* I was interviewing her.
ENDICOTT. *(At phone)* Gimme the City desk— *What* was he doing to her?
WILSON. And with the shade down?
MURPHY. *(Enters. Crossing down Center, picking up phone)* Where the hell you been, Hildy? There's the damnedest Hallowe'en going on—the whole police force standing on its ear. *(He sits in chair Left, back of table)* Murphy talking. Gimme the desk.

(KRUGER *enters.)*

ENDICOTT. Well the old bird wasn't
out there. Don't know where we're going next. Call you later. *(Crosses Right
and sits in his chair.)*                    *(Together.)*
WILSON. Wilson speaking. No luck
yet on Williams. Call you back.

KRUGER. *(Through babble)* God, I never was so
tired in my life!

(KRUGER *crosses down Left. Sits.*)

HILDY. Any news?

MURPHY. This is Murphy— Well, they surrounded
the house, only Williams wasn't there.

McCUE. *(Enters. Crossing to phone on his table)*
God, what a chase!

MURPHY. *(Into phone)* Wait a minute. They shot
somebody, anyhow!

KRUGER. Gimme a rewrite.

MURPHY. Herman Schulte, the Sheriff's brother-in-
law. He was leading the squad through the house, and
was looking under a bed when Deputy John F. Watson
came in the room and mistook him for Earl. Shot him
right in the pants. Yeah, a bull's eye. Right! *(Hangs up.)*

HILDY. *(Taking cue, "A bull's eye")* He always had
lead in his pants.

McCUE. *(At his phone)* McCue talking. Gimme the
desk!

KRUGER. *(Phoning too)* This is Kruger, out with
Hartman's deputies— Yeah—I'm in the drug store, at
Clark and Fullerton. Well, call me back if you don't
believe me. *(Hangs up.)*

McCUE. That so? I'll check on it. *(Hangs up)* There's
something doing at Harrison Street Station. *(Jiggles
hook)* Gimme Harrison 2500. Hurry it, will you
please?

KRUGER. *(To* MOLLIE, *who is in the swivel chair in
front of the desk)* What's the idea, Mollie? Can't you
flop somewhere else?

MURPHY. Yah, parking her fanny in here like it was her house. *(Takes a sniff of the air)* Fleur de Floozie, she's got on.

KRUGER. Nnch! *(Neighing like a horse.)*

MURPHY. Go on, Mollie, put it somewhere else. Go out and stink up Clark Street.

MOLLIE. You lay off me!

McCUE. Look out—she'll start bawling again. *(In phone)* I'll hold the wire. Only don't forget me.

HILDY. *(Taking cue, "start bawling again")* Let her alone fellas. She's not doing anything. *(He crosses Left to cooler.)*

*(Together.)*

MURPHY. *(To HILDY)* What are you two so chummy about?

ENDICOTT. Yah, they were locked in here together when he come along.

WILSON. Wouldn't open the door.

McCUE. You'll be out of training for your honeymoon—playing pinochle with this baby.

MURPHY. I thought you were going to catch a train?

KRUGER. Yah—he was running around here a few minutes ago with his pants on fire about going to New York.

*(MOLLIE is futilely trying to powder her nose.)*

ENDICOTT. Told us he was interviewing her.

MURPHY. What are you trying to do? Scoop us?

HILDY. I'm waiting here for Walter. He's coming over with some dough.

McCUE. *(Into phone)* Hello, Sarge. McCue. I hear you got a tip on Williams?

WILSON. Look, she's got the snakes. What you making faces about?

ENDICOTT. *(Almost singing it)* She's jealous because Hildy's going to be married.

HILDY. *(Touching her shoulder)* Go on— Show 'em you can smile through your tears. Relax.

MOLLIE. *(Jumping away)* You let me alone—all of you.

(SCHWARTZ *enters.*)

McCUE. *(Into phone)* Yeah? What's the address?

SCHWARTZ. Hello, fellas. What the hell, Hildy? You still here?

ENDICOTT. Yah, and trying to hang something on us? If you ask me. Come on, Hildy! Give us the low-down!

SCHWARTZ. *(Turning to window)* Who pulled these shades down? *(He crosses to window up Right and pulls up shade.)*

McCUE. *(Standing up)* Hey! This looks good. An old lady just called up the detective bureau and claims Williams is hiding under her piazza.

MURPHY. *(Rising)* Who you got there?

McCUE. The Captain.

MURPHY. *(Crosses and takes phone. McCUE crosses Right)* Let me talk to him. Hello, Turkey— How's your gussie mollio? I hear this guy Williams is hiding in your mustache—yah? (MOLLIE *crosses her legs)* Well, get your nose out of the way. *(Hangs up. Points to* MOLLIE'S *crossed and highly visible legs)* Oooh! Lookit! Pike's Peak! *(He crosses and sits at big table.)*

McCUE. Listen, fellows, that sounds like a pretty good tip. What do you say?

HILDY. *(Crossing to Right edge of desk)* If you boys want to go out, I'll cover this end for you.

ENDICOTT. Aw, the hell with chasing around any more. I spent a dollar forty on taxis already.

KRUGER. Don't let's do any more going out.

SCHWARTZ. *(Turning to group)* If you ask me, I got a hunch Williams ain't anywheres they been looking for him.

WILSON. How do you mean?

SCHWARTZ. Well, I just been talking to Jacobi, about that roof he's supposed to have jumped off of. Look! *(McCue goes Right to window)* Now there's that skylight he got out of.

ENDICOTT. Where? *(He gets up and goes to lower window. Pulls up shade.)*

McCUE. How could he get from there to the ground?

SCHWARTZ. That's just the point. *(He turns back into the room)* Jacobi's gone up there with a couple of cops to look over the whole roof.

McCUE. *(Leaning out)* I tell you what he could have done, though. Look! He could have jumped over to this roof. That's only about four feet. *(He turns to room for corroboration.)*

ENDICOTT. *(Out of window)* Yeh, he could have done that all right.

KRUGER. I'm pretending there ain't no Earl Williams.

SCHWARTZ. *(A step into room)* And that's why I'm telling you guys that I don't think this guy Williams is anywhere they been looking for him. I got a stinking hunch he's right in this building.

(MOLLIE *drops vanity case.)*

HILDY. *(Derisive)* Hanging around like a duck in a shootin' gallery. (MOLLIE *picks up vanity case.)* I suppose. You're a lot of bright guys—

McCUE. *(Crossing Center)* It'd be easy once he got on this roof—

HILDY. Hey—Sherlock Holmes, what correspondence school did you graduate from?

SCHWARTZ. What's the matter with that? (KRUGER *rises.)* He could come down on the rain pipe and crawl into any one of those windows on this side—

KRUGER. *(Crossing Right, lazily)* Well, if the story's going to walk right in the window—

HILDY. The master minds at work! (BENSINGER *enters.)* Why don't you guys go home—he'll probably call on you—

BENSINGER. *(Approaching his desk.* MOLLIE's *sitting in his chair, hidden from him at the moment by* HILDY) Hello, Hildy. Thought you were going to New York? *(*HILDY *has sprung into action with* BENSINGER's *entrance, but* BENSINGER *sees* MOLLIE) For God's sake, what's she doing in my chair? (*MOLLIE *springs up.)* Is that the only place you can sit? That's my property and I don't want anybody using it!

(MOLLIE *backs down Left and sits in chair.)*

HILDY. *(Brushing off the chair)* Nobody's using it, Roy. *(He helps* BENSINGER *to sit down and stands just to the Left of him)* Everything's all right.

BENSINGER. Any of you fellows got some aspirin?

ENDICOTT. *(Turning from window)* No, sweetheart, but I got some nice cyanide.

(KRUGER *sits Right.)*

BENSINGER. Cut the kidding, fellows. I tell you I'm sick.

SCHWARTZ. How about a good truss? I'll sell it to you cheap.

HILDY. What's the matter, Roy? Off your feed?

BENSINGER. If I haven't got a good case of grippe coming, I miss my guess. *(Reaching for desk cover)* Get out of the way, will you?

HILDY. *(Patting his shoulder)* I hope you didn't get it off me.

BENSINGER. I got it off somebody. Everybody using my phone all the time—it's a wonder I ain't caught anything worse. *(Pushing* HILDY *slightly)* Look out, I got to get my cup.

HILDY. *(Doubling up as if in agony)* Wait a minute, will you?—Oh!

BENSINGER. What's the matter?

HILDY. I don't know—oh—

BENSINGER. Don't you feel all right?

HILDY. No. *(Coughs violently in* BENSINGER'S *face.)*

BENSINGER. *(Jumps up, crosses Center wiping his mouth with a handkerchief)* Don't do that!

HILDY. *(Weakly)* Do what?

BENSINGER. Cough on a guy! Yes!

HILDY. *(Crossing Center)* Well, I don't know what's the matter. I suddenly got a pain right— *(Vaguely indicates his throat)* —and a kind of rash on my chest. *(Opens his shirt.)*

BENSINGER. *(Recoiling)* What? You've probably got some disease.

MURPHY. Sure! He's got the pazooza!

HILDY. *(Advancing on* BENSINGER; *takes his hand and presses it against his forehead)* Feel? Ain't that fever?

BENSINGER. Hey, cut it out! It may be diptheria!

HILDY. I woke up this morning and had yellow spots all over my stomach—

BENSINGER. *(Backing up Right above table)* Now, this ain't funny.

(HILDY *following* BENSINGER. *Seizes* BENSINGER.)

KRUGER. For God's sake, Roy, can't you see he's kidding you!

BENSINGER. *(As soon as* HILDY *touches him)* Let go of me! *(He backs Right)* You may have something contagious! If you're sick go to a hospital! (HILDY *coughs in his face.)* For the love of God! *(He ducks around* HILDY *up Left of him.)*

MURPHY. It's no worse than a bad cold, Roy.

HILDY. *(Opening his mouth)* Can you see anything in there? Aaah!

BENSINGER. Listen, fellows! You ain't got any sense, letting him hang around here. We'll all catch it, whatever it is! *(They* ALL *laugh.* HILDY *still clings to him.)* All right, laugh! But I'm going to get Doc Springer and clean this whole place up! You God damn maniacs! *(He tears free from* HILDY *and rushes out.*

HILDY *bursts into hysterical laugh and crosses Left, leaning against desk.)*

ENDICOTT. What's the idea, Hildy? Now he'll be burning sulphur for a week like last time—

McCUE. *(Crossing Left Center to* HILDY) Yeah, you're leavin', but we gotta work here, with all them stink pots— What a sense of humor you got.

SCHWARTZ. You look here— What about Williams? Let's get the cops and search the building. What do you say?

ENDICOTT. I could use that reward—

MURPHY. You'd never get past the basement.

McCUE. Gee, it would be funny if we found him right here in the building.

SCHWARTZ. What do you say? Should we get the cops?

MURPHY. Call up Lieutenant Callahan, Mac. Tell him we got a hot tip.

HILDY. *(Taking cue, "Mac," he grabs* McCUE) Wait! What do you want to call the cops for? Suppose he *is* in the building. They'll grab all the reward and you guys won't get a smell.

SCHWARTZ. Huh?

WILSON. That's right.

HILDY. Listen. Each of us take a floor. (MRS. GRANT *enters.)* and whoever finds him, we split it up. What do you say? (MRS. GRANT *crosses Left Center to* HILDY, *who is backing away)* Now, now, listen, Mother—

MRS. GRANT. Don't you Mother me! If you've got anything to say for yourself you come downstairs and say it to Peggy—

HILDY. *(Turning to* MRS. GRANT) Listen, Mother, tell Peggy I'll be downstairs in five minutes, will you? Will you go down and tell her that?

MRS. GRANT. *(Taking cue, "five minutes")* No, sir— I don't move out of here without you.

HILDY. Listen, Mother, you don't understand. Now I told Peggy—

MRS. GRANT. I know what you told her. A lot of gibberish about a murderer!

(MOLLIE *rises.*)

HILDY. No—no!
MRS. GRANT. I don't care if you *did* catch him, you come with me this minute! } *(Together.)*

ENDICOTT. *(Taking cue, "you did catch him")* I knew there was something in the wind.

MURPHY. *(Jumping up and taking cue, "there was something")* Who says he caught him? What's going on here?

McCUE. *(Taking cue, "says he caught him?")* What do you mean caught a murderer?

KRUGER. So that's it, is it?

SCHWARTZ. *(Taking cue, "what do you mean")* Did she say caught a murderer?

WILSON. *(Rising and taking cue, "did she say")* What's that? Caught a murderer?

(WOODENSHOES *enters, stands listening.*)

HILDY. No, no! I don't know what she's talking about! I didn't tell her any such thing.

MRS. GRANT. Yes you did!
MOLLIE. He never told her that! } *(Together.)*

(MURPHY *starts to cross Left.* ENDICOTT *advances Center.*)

HILDY. I said I was trying to catch one, that's all! You got it balled up, Mother!

(SCHWARTZ *crosses Center.*)

MURPHY. *(To* MOLLIE*)* What do *you* know about it? How do you know he didn't, huh? (MURPHY *grabs* MOLLIE'S *arm.*)

MOLLIE. *(Backing down Left)* Let go of my arm!

ENDICOTT. *(A step Left)* Hildy and that tart were in here together!

HILDY. *(Crosses Left, to MURPHY)* Say, lay off her!

WILSON. I thought something was going on!

WOODENSHOES. *(Crosses down Center)* Yah! Yah! She's the one that knows? Ask *her!*

MURPHY. *(Wheeling on him)* What do you mean—knows?

WOODENSHOES. *(Pointing)* Serchay la femme! *(To MOLLIE)* Where's Earl Williams?

MOLLIE. *(Laughing lamely)* How the hell should I know?

WOODENSHOES. Where have you got him, kid?

MURPHY. *(Turning on HILDY)* Who you holding out on, Hildy? Come clean, or God damn it, we'll knock it out of you!

*(SCHWARTZ, McCUE, MURPHY and ENDICOTT rush at HILDY and push him over desk. MRS. GRANT backs up Center.)*

SCHWARTZ. Sock him.

McCUE. Yeah. What the hell! Sock him, Jimmie!                *(Together.)*

ENDICOTT. You dirty double-crosser! We'll murder you!

MOLLIE. *(Crosses Center, then turns)* Wait! You damned stool pigeons! He don't know where Earl Williams is! I'm the one that knows!

McCUE. *(Turning around)* Knows?                *(Together.)*

ENDICOTT. *(A step Center)* What do you mean you know?

*(The REPORTERS leave HILDY and turn on MOLLIE.)*

WOODENSHOES. Where is he?

MOLLIE. Go find out, you lousy heels. You don't think I'm going to tell?

WOODENSHOES. You'll tell all right! We'll make you
tell!

MOLLIE. *(Slowly backing up Center)* Yeah? Yeah?
The hell I will.

HILDY. Let her alone. She's goofy.

(SCHWARTZ *and* ENDICOTT *turn.* MOLLIE *makes a sudden lunge for the door, but* WILSON *gets there
ahead of her. She backs down Right.)*

SCHWARTZ. Look out!   } *(Together.)*
ENDICOTT. Close that door!}

MURPHY. *(Taking cue, "that door")* Don't let her
get away!

McCUE. You ain't getting out of here, Mollie.

ENDICOTT. *(Advancing on her)* Now where is he?
In the building?

McCUE. *(Advancing on her)* Where are you hiding
him?

MOLLIE. *(Back down Right))* I ain't going to squeal!
I ain't going to squeal!

MURPHY. *(Crossing Center)* Come on, you lousy
tart! Before we kick your teeth out!

ENDICOTT. You want us to call the cops and give you
the boots?

MURPHY. Go on, Woodenshoes! Slap it out of her!

WOODENSHOES. *(Grabs her)* Come on now! Where is
he before I hurt you!

MOLLIE. *(Wrenching free)* Take your hands off me!
*(She picks up* ENDICOTT'S *chair; swings it in a vicious
circle to ward off the oncoming* REPORTERS) Let me
alone or I'll break your God damn heads!

ENDICOTT. Put down that chair!

SCHWARTZ. *(Sneaking Center below table)* Get
around—get on the side of her!

MOLLIE. *(Backing off, threateningly)* No, you don't!
Keep away from me!

(WALTER BURNS *enters. Stands up Center.)*

KRUGER. Grab her!

*(The MEN are closing in on her.)*

MOLLIE. You'll never get it out of me! *(She throws
the chair at McCUE and ENDICOTT)* Never!

McCUE. Look out! ⎤
MURPHY. For God's sake! ⎥ *(Together taking busi-*
ENDICOTT. Hold her! ⎥ *ness cue of the chair*
HILDY. Mollie! ⎦ *being thrown.)*

*(MOLLIE runs for the lower window sill; jumps out
of the window. There is a moment's pause. The
REPORTERS rush to the window. ALL except
SCHWARTZ who runs out. HILDY dashes over
too. MRS. GRANT crosses Center, sinks into
SCHWARTZ'S chair weeping.)*

McCUE. *(As he rushes up to window)* ⎤
Mother of God! ⎥
MURPHY. *(Rushing to window)* What ⎥
do you think of that? ⎥
SCHWARTZ. *(Exiting)* My God, she's ⎥
dead! ⎥
KRUGER. *(Rushing to window)* Oh my ⎥ *(Together.)*
God, what has she done? ⎥
WOODENSHOES. *(Exiting)* I never ⎥
thought she'd do that! That's terrible. ⎥
MRS. GRANT. Take me out of here! ⎥
Take me out of here! Oh my God! ⎥
WILSON. *(Exiting)* No, she's moving. ⎦
Get the cops, Woodenshoes!
HILDY. *(At window)* Holy God, the poor kid. Poor
kid!

*(VOICES come from the jailyard: "Hey, Carl!" "Get
a doctor!" "Who was it?" "What happened?"
etc.)*

McCue. *(Exiting)* What do you think
of her doing that?

Kruger. *(Exiting)* If she's killed herself, we'll never find out.      } *(Together.)*

Murphy. *(Exiting)* Yes, that's a
twenty-foot jump. She's killed herself
sure.

Wilson. *(Off)* Wasn't that the God damndest thing?

(Hildy, *a little dazed, is still on stage.* Walter *is
standing near the door.* Mrs. Grant *is prostrate
in a chair.*)

Endicott. *(He rushes off)* She ain't killed! Hey!

(Walter *slams door.*)

Hildy. *(Turning)* Walter! Did you see that?

Walter. Yeah. Where is he?

Hildy. *(Back to window)* She jumped out of the
window!

Walter. I know. Where is he, I said?

Hildy. *(Looking out of the window)* She's moving!
Thank God, she ain't killed herself!

Walter. Come to, Hildy! Where have you got
Williams?

Hildy. *(Turning, but still absorbed in the* Mollie
*matter)* Huh? He's— He's in the desk. *(As* Walter
*crosses to desk, he turns to window again)* Thank
God, she ain't dead.

(Walter *opens desk a crack.*)

Earl. Let me out! I can't stand it!

Walter. Keep quiet! You're sitting pretty. *(He
slams desk.)*

Mrs. Grant. *(Has observed this, jumps up)* What's
the matter?

Walter. Who the hell is that?

*(He crosses up Center and opens door signalling* TONY *and* LOUIE *to come in.)*

MRS. GRANT. What are you doing? Oh, my God!

WALTER. *(Comes down Left Center)* Shut up!

MRS. GRANT. *(Crossing Left Center)* I won't shut up!! That girl killed herself. Oh! You're doing something wrong. What's in there?

WALTER. Louie! Take her out of here, will you?

*(*LOUIE *and* TONY *come down Left and Right of* MRS. GRANT *respectively.)*

MRS. GRANT. What did you say?

WALTER. Take her over to Polack Mike's, and lock her up. Tell 'em it's a case of delirium tremens.

LOUIE. *(Calls)* Hey Tony!

MRS. GRANT. *(Screaming)* Don't touch me!

LOUIE. Tony, give me a hand with this lady.

*(They drag* MRS. GRANT *out.* HILDY *suddenly turns, and dashes around table.)*

HILDY. *(Taking cue, "touch me")* Listen, Walter, this'll get me in a hell of a jam— (*TONY has a hand over* MRS. GRANT's *mouth)* Now don't worry, Mother, this is only temporary— Honest to God, Walter—

*(They drag her out.* WALTER *closes door.* HILDY *dashes at him, and they crash together at the door.)*

WALTER. *(Throwing him away)* Where do you think you're going?

HILDY. *(Dashing at* WALTER *again)* Let go of me! I gotta get my girl! She's downstairs in a cab all alone.

WALTER. *(Throwing him away again)* Your girl! Good God, what are you? Some puking college boy! Why, in time of war you could be shot for what you're doing—for less than you're doing!

HILDY. To hell with you—there's your story—locked up in that desk. Smear it all over the front page— Earl Williams caught by the *Examiner*, and take all the credit— I covered your story and I covered it God damn right— Now I'm gettin'—out— *(He dashes harder than ever at* WALTER.*)*

WALTER. *(Throwing him away)* You drolling saphead— What do you mean—story? You've got the whole city by the seat of the pants.

HILDY. I know all about that, but—

WALTER. *(Grabs his arm)* You know hell—you got the brains of a pancake—listen, Hildy, if I didn't have your interest at heart would I be wastin' time now arguin' with you? You've done somethin' big—you've stepped into a new class—

HILDY. Huh?

WALTER. *(Pulling him down Center)* Listen, we'll make such monkeys out of those ward heelers that nobody will vote for them—not even their *wives*.

HILDY. *(Breaking away)* Expose 'em, huh—

WALTER. Expose 'em! Crucify 'em! We're gonna keep Williams under cover till morning so's the *Examiner* can break the story exclusive— Then we'll let the Senator in on the capture—share the glory with him.

HILDY. I see—I see. *(Blinking and warming up.)*

WALTER. You've kicked over the whole City Hall like an applecart. This ain't a newspaper story—it's a career.

HILDY. *(Coming up to* WALTER) Gee, I—I wasn't figuring it that way, I guess. We'll be the white-haired boys, won't we?

WALTER. Why, they'll be naming streets after you. You and I and the Senator, are going to *run* this town —do you understand that?

HILDY. Yeah—yeah! But—wait a minute—we can't leave Williams here— One of these reporters'll—

WALTER. We're going to take him over to my pri-

vate office right away. Where's the *Examiner* pl.
*(He turns up Center.)*

HILDY. That one. The red one. (WALTER *crosses down Right Center.* HILDY *crosses Center)* How you gonna do it? They'll see him!

WALTER. Not if he's inside the desk— We'll carry the desk over. *(Into phone)* Hello! *Examiner,* give me Duffy Cornell— *(To* HILDY) I'd have had him there now if you hadn't given me such an argument.

HILDY. *(Looking at desk)* You can't take that out. It's crawling with cops outside.

WALTER. We'll lower it out of the window *with pulleys. (Into phone)* Quit stallin'. *(To* HILDY) Hildy! Get that machine and start pounding out a lead, will you— Come on—snap into it—

HILDY. *(Crosses Center, hunts for paper)* How much you want on it—?

WALTER. All the words you got—

HILDY. *(Crossing to desk)* Where's some paper?

WALTER. *(Into phone)* Hello—hello!

HILDY. *(Pulls out Johnson & Johnson Red Cross supplies)* Can I call the Mayor an animal at bay?

WALTER. Call him a nigger if you want to! *(Into phone)* Come on! Come on!

HILDY. *(Finding two scripts)* How about the time he had his house painted by the Fire Department?

WALTER. Give him the works— *(Into phone)* Hello, Duffy! Get set! We got the biggest story in the world. Earl Williams caught by the *Examiner*—exclusive.

HILDY. *(Finds a hot water bottle)* Oh, for God's sake! *(Gets the paper in a blue folder. Starts tearing folder off. Crosses Center.)*

WALTER. *(Into phone)* Duffy! Send down word to Butch McGuirk I want ten huskies from the circulation department to lam right over here— (HILDY *grabs* SCHWARTZ's *chair and puts it at end of table. Then crosses up Center for typewriter)* press room Criminal Court Building. That's what I said— Butch McGuirk.

Now listen, Duffy— (HILDY *takes cover off typewriter*) I want you to tear out the whole front page— (HILDY *picks up typewriter.* PEGGY *enters*) Johnson's writing the lead now.

PEGGY. Hildy!

WALTER. *(Turning)* What the hell do you want?

PEGGY. Hildy!

HILDY. What?

WALTER. Listen, Miss, you can't come in here! *(Into phone)* To hell with the Chinese earthquake! What's that?

HILDY. *(Taking cue, "the Chinese earthquake")* Listen, darling—

PEGGY. Where's Mother?

WALTER. *(Into phone)* I don't care if there's a million dead!

HILDY. Peggy, I got to ask you to do something! A big favor.

PEGGY. *(Divining)* You're not coming?

HILDY. Now don't get sore and fly off the handle, darling. What happened was—

PEGGY. You're *not! Are* you? Tell me, Hildy! Tell me the truth!

WALTER. *(Into phone. Taking cue, "not coming")* Take all those Miss America pictures off page six. *(To* PEGGY) Now look here, little girl—

PEGGY. *(Wheels on* WALTER) You're doing this to him! He was going and you stopped him!

HILDY. *(Taking cue, "Doing this to him")* Something terrific's happened, Peggy— Wait till I tell you! I couldn't—

WALTER. *(Taking cue, "Tell you")* You'll tell her nothing! She's a woman, you damn fool!

PEGGY. Well, I'm not going to let you do it! You're coming right now! With me! *(She grabs typewriter.)*

WALTER. Holy God!

HILDY. But it's the biggest chance of my life. Now listen, darling—

WALTER. *(Taking cue, "of my life")* Shut up, will you?

PEGGY. *(Lets go of typewriter)* You don't *want* to marry me! That's all!

HILDY. *(Puts down typewriter on big table)* That ain't true! Just because you won't listen you're saying I don't love you when you know I'd cut off my hands for you! I'd do anything in the world for you! Anything! *(WARN Curtain.)*

WALTER. *(Turns back to phone on* HILDY's *"cut off my hands for you," and takes that as cue)* What?— What's that?—To hell with the League of Nations! Spike it?

PEGGY. You never intended to be decent and live like a human being! You were lying all the time!

HILDY. *(Backs to Center)* Peggy, don't keep saying that!

WALTER. *(Over the phone, without a break in the* PEGGY-HILDY *scene)* What's that? What?

*(Together.)*

PEGGY. *(Crossing Center towards* HILDY*)* Lying! That's what you were! Just lying!

HILDY. All right! If that's what you think!

WALTER. *(To them)* H. Sebastian God! I'm trying to concentrate! *(He motions with phone.)*

PEGGY. *(Taking cue, "God")* I see what you are now! You're just a bum! Like him— *(Indicates* WALTER) And all the rest!

HILDY. Sure! That's what I am! All right!

WALTER. *(Into phone. Suddenly screaming)* No! Leave the rooster story alone—that's human interest!

PEGGY. You're just a heartless selfish animal without any feelings! *(Turns to* WALTER *viciously)* And you're worse! It's all your fault, and if you think I'm going to put up with it— *(She grabs his arm.)*

WALTER. *(He shakes her off, she falls against the table back to audience)* Shut up, will you?

*(EARL starts to open the desk.)*

HILDY. Yeah! That's what I am! A bum! Without any feelings!! And that's all I want to be! *(He sees* WILLIAMS, *dashes over and slams desk shut)* Get back in there you God damn turtle!

PEGGY. *(Rushing off)* You never did love me or you couldn't talk to me like that!

HILDY. *(Not stopping for* PEGGY's *line)* And if you want me you'll have to take me as I am instead of trying to turn me into some la-de-da with a cane! *(He slams the door and crosses down Center)* I'm no stuffed shirt, writing peanut ads! *(He sits—starts typing.)*

WALTER. *(Into phone. Taking cue, "a bum")* Hello. The edition gone in yet?—Well, don't! Never mind the mail trains! What? *What!* You're not working for the advertising department—no! To hell with Marshall Field! You stick on this phone!

## CURTAIN

# ACT THREE

SCENE: *The same. Five minutes later.*
*The shades are drawn but the lights on full up.*
HILDY, *smoking, is typing furiously.* WALTER
*is pacing up and down. He crosses Left. Looks at
watch. Listens at desk. Crosses up to door. Looks
out, closes and locks door. Crosses down to table.
He finally picks up receiver, which has been standing on the table.*

WALTER. Duffy—Duffy! *(To* HILDY*)* God damn it!
I told him to stay on that phone. If I had a few people
who did what they were told I could get something ac-
complished— I bet he never told 'em to take taxis—
*(Crosses Right to window)* Butch and the gang are
probably *walking* over here— *(Looks out of window)*
Oh, for Chri— Now the moon's—out! (HILDY *types
on regardless.* WALTER *goes to the desk and raps three
times.* EARL *taps back three times)* Fine! Three taps
is me! Don't forget— You're sitting pretty now. Got
enough air? *(He raises the roll top an inch or two and
fans air in with his hand. Closes it again)* Is that better?
*(Closing the desk and crossing to phone)* Lam into 'em,
Hildy! Below the belt! Every punch! *(Into phone, with
great sarcasm)* Hello!—Duffy, where you been? Well,
the hell with your diabetes; you stick on this phone!
Listen, did you impress it on Butch to take taxis—that
every minute counts? Who's he bringing with him?
What do you mean, you don't know! But you told him it
was life and death, huh? All right, stick on this wire!
*(Putting down receiver, he crosses Center)* Duffy's
getting old— Well, Butch is on the way, Hildy— All
we got to do is hold out for fifteen minutes—

HILDY. The boys'll be back. They'll be coming in to phone.

WALTER. *(Pacing up and down Center)* I'll handle them. It's that three-toed Sheriff I'm worrying about. If he starts sticking his snoot into this— *(Turns to* HILDY) I wonder if we could arrest him for anything? (HILDY *is typing again)* Did you ever get the dope on that stenographer he seduced?

HILDY. *(Stops, thinks)* That was the Coroner.

WALTER. Haven't we got *any*thing on him—besides graft?

HILDY. *(Thoughtfully, puffing)* He's got an idiot kid in the asylum.

WALTER. I don't see how we can use that against him— No—wait a minute. Idiot kid. Idiot kid. *(Thinking)* No, that's impractical— *(Crosses Left and then turns to* HILDY) What's your lead?

HILDY. *(Shuffles through papers. Then reads)* "While hundreds of Sheriff Hartman's paid gunmen stalked through Chicago shooting innocent bystanders, spreading their reign of terror, Earl Williams was lurking less than twenty yards from the Sheriff's office when—"

WALTER. *(Crossing above* HILDY) That's *lousy!* Aren't you going to mention the *Examiner?* Don't we take *any* credit?

HILDY. I'm putting that in the second paragraph—

WALTER. Who the hell's going to read the second paragraph? Ten years I've been telling you how to write a newspaper story— My God, have I got to do everything? Get the story! Write the story?

HILDY. Listen, you poor manaic! I can blow better newspaper stories out of my nose than you can write!

WALTER. *(Sarcastically)* "While hundreds of paid gunmen are out taking a walk"— God, that stinks! *(He crosses to window down Right)* You ought to get back to chasing pictures.

HILDY. Yeah?

WALTER. *(Peeking out)* You were good at that!

HILDY. Why, you ungrateful hound. Who wrote the Fitzgerald confession? Who wrote Ruth Randolph's diary? And how about the Dayton flood? Even the telegraph operator was crying!

WALTER. All right, make me cry now! *(He crosses to "Examiner" phone)* Duffy! Listen, Duffy. What's the name of that religious editor of ours? The fellow with the dirty collar? Sipper what? Well, where is he? What do you mean you don't know where one of our most important men is? Well, you get a hold of him and tell him I want to see him right away! *(To* HILDY*)* Do you know what I'm gonna do?

HILDY. Oh, shut up, or I'll throw this typewriter at your head!

WALTER. *(Happily)* I'm going to get the Reverend Sipperly to make up a prayer for the City of Chicago—right across the top of the paper!—*(He crosses Center)* "Our Father Who art in Heaven"— "There were four hundred and twenty-one murders in Chicago last year!" All in religious lingo, see? Eight columns Old English boldface! The God damnedest prayer you ever heard— *(He crosses back to "Examiner" phone)* God, what an idea!

HILDY. You better pray that this desk will float out of the window over to the paper.

WALTER. Wait a minute, Hildy— *(Looking over his shoulder)* Wait, wait, wait, wait—I got an inspiration! Now take this down, just as I say it! *(He pulls a page from the typewriter and crumples it in his hand. Then lays a clean sheet on the typewriter.)*

HILDY. *(Jumping up)* Some day you're going to do that, Walter, and I'm gonna belt you on the jaw—! You God damn know-it-all! *(He grabs the crumpled paper from* WALTER.*)*

WALTER. *(Claps his hand and crosses Center, pacing)* Here's the way to start this story! Here's your lead: "*The Chicago Examiner* again rode to the rescue of the city last night in the darkest hour of her history! Earl Williams, the—" *(A furtive look at the desk stops him. He crosses Center and whispers to* HILDY) "Earl Williams, the Bolshevik tiger who leaped snarling from the gallows upon the flanks of the city was captured—"

HILDY. *(Turning to typewriter)* I got you, I got you—

WALTER. Go on from *there!*

(HILDY *is hurriedly putting another sheet into the machine, as the DOOR KNOB is rattled.)*

HILDY. *(Turning to door)* What do you want to do?

BENSINGER'S VOICE. *(Outside)* What's the idea of locking this door?

HILDY. That's Bensinger. That's his desk.

WALTER. What's his name again?

*(The DOOR KNOB is rattled violently.)*

HILDY. Bensinger. Reporter from the *Tribune*—Covers the building.

BENSINGER'S VOICE. *(Outside)* Open this door, will you? Who's in there?

WALTER. *(Crossing up Center)* I'll handle him! The *Tribune*, eh? Watch me.

*(Goes to door. He opens the door.* BENSINGER *appears.* WALTER *crosses down Left.)*

BENSINGER. *(Entering)* Ain't you got any more sense than to— *(Sees* WALTER. *He takes off his hat)* Oh, hello, Mr. Burns— Why, quite an honor, having you come over here.

WALTER. *(Turning to* BENSINGER. *Warmly)* Hello, Bensinger.

BENSINGER. *(Crosses Left to* WALTER*)* Excuse me. I just want to—

WALTER. *(Stopping him)* Quite a coincidence, my running into you tonight, isn't it, Hildy?

HILDY. *(Begins to proof-read his story)* Yeah.

BENSINGER. How do you mean?

WALTER. I was having a little chat about you just this afternoon—with Duffy Cornell.

BENSINGER. Is that so? *(Essaying the pleasantry)* Nothing detrimental, I hope.

WALTER. I should say not. (BENSINGER *smiles, starts towards desk again.* WALTER *stops him)* That was one swell story you had in the paper this morning.

BENSINGER. Well, I'm glad you think so, Mr. Burns. Did you care for the poem?

WALTER. The poem? The poem was great. I got a big kick out of that.

BENSINGER. *(Diverted by such sweet words)* Did you like the ending? *(He recites)*

"and all is well, outside his cell
But in his heart he hears
The hangman calling, and the gallows falling,
And his white-haired mother's tears—"

WALTER. *(Overcome)* It's heartbreaking! Look here, Bensinger, how would you like to work for me?

BENSINGER. What!

WALTER. I mean it. We need somebody like you. All we got now is a lot of lowbrows. Like Johnson here. *(Pushing BENSINGER farther from the desk)* I tell you what you do. Go over and talk to Duffy now. I just had him on the phone. You'll catch him, if you hurry.

BENSINGER. You mean seriously, Mr. Burns?

WALTER. *(Crosses to "Examiner" phone)* I'll show you how serious I am. *(He turns, grabs BENSINGER's sleeve, and drags him down Right Center to the phone. Into phone)* Duffy! I'm sending Bensinger over to see you. *(To BENSINGER)* Marvin, isn't it?

BENSINGER. No, Roy. Roy V.

WALTER. Funny I should forget that! *(Into phone)* Roy Bensinger, the poet. Put him right on the staff!

BENSINGER. Right away, you mean?

WALTER. *(Into phone)* Never mind what doing— He'll tell you. No, I'll talk salary with him right here.

*(To* BENSINGER*)* How much you getting on the *Tribune,* Roy?

BENSINGER. Seventy-five.

WALTER. All right, I'll give you a hundred and a by-line. *(Into phone)* He's to get a hundred and a by-line, Duffy. Tell the cashier. Let him have everything he wants. No! He can use the big desk in the corner. *(He puts down phone and crosses Center)* Now look here, Bensinger. I'll tell you what I want you to do. *(He turns to* BENSINGER*)* I want you to hustle right over to the office and tell Duffy I've—I've assigned you to write the human interest side of the manhunt. I want it from the point of view of the escaped man. *(Acting it out)* He hides, cowering—afraid of every light, *(He crosses up Right to* BENSINGER*)* or every sound—hears footsteps—his heart going like that. And all the time they're closing in— *(Taps his chest)* get the sense of an animal at bay!

BENSINGER. Sort of a Jack London style?

WALTER. Exactly. *(He pushes* BENSINGER *toward the door)* Now you ain't got a minute to lose. Hop right over to the office.

BENSINGER. *(Turning slowly)* Well, I don't know about quittin' the *Tribune* that way, Mr. Burns. It's not quite ethical—

WALTER. What did they ever do for you?—They've never considered your interests—that is, from what I hear—

BENSINGER. Well, between you and me, they have given me a pretty rotten deal. The way they handle my copy's a shame—just butcher it.

WALTER. *(His hand in the air)* Your copy will be sacred on the *Examiner.* I guarantee that personally—

BENSINGER. You can't lop off the end of a story and get the same effect. The whole *feeling* goes—

(HILDY *puts down his copy, and sits, head in hands.)*

WALTER. Of course. Now I want a real Bensinger

story tomorrow morning, with a crackerjack poem on the side. *(He has him nearly to the door.)*

BENSINGER. *(Starting, crossing Left)* I left my rhyming dictionary in the desk.

WALTER. *(Stopping him)* Wait a minute! It don't have to rhyme! *(He opens the door and starts to push him out)* Now duck!

BENSINGER. *(Turning in doorway)* Gee, I'm terribly grateful, Mr. Burns. Do you suppose there might be an opening some time as foreign correspondent? I parlay a little in French, you know.

WALTER. *(Starting to close door)* That'll all depend on yourself. I'll keep you in mind.

BENSINGER. *(Leaving—a happy child. He waves his hand, puts on his hat and exits)* Well, au revoir, mon capitaine!

WALTER. *(He starts to close door, gets an idea. Opens it and calls out)* Bon jour! *(WALTER closes the door and skips to the "Examiner" phone)* Duffy! Listen! Now get this! A God damn *Tribune* sneak is coming over to get a job. Yeah, Bensinger, the fellow I told you about. Now, listen, handle him with kid gloves and tell him to get busy writing poetry. No—no! We don't want him but wait till he gets through. Then tell him his poetry stinks and kick him down the stairs— *(Receiver down. He crosses up Right Center. Locks door)* His white-haired mother's tears! *(He crosses Left and taps three times on desk. Three taps answer)* Attaboy! You can't go wrong! *(He turns to* HILDY) Come on, Hildy, tear into it! Don't sit there like a frozen robin!

HILDY. You've just messed up my whole life! That's what you've done!

WALTER. *(To Right of desk)* Listen, Hildy. We ought to have our plans all set when Butch gets here. All we can look for out of that guy is pure, peasant strength— A mental blank, *(Sentimentally)* but he'd go through hell for me! *(He looks at desk. Then at window.)*

HILDY. What a fine horse's bustle I turned out to be!

WALTER. The window's out— *(He crosses down Left)* We'll have him pick it up and walk right out of the building with it. With ten guys it'll be a cinch.

HILDY. She was the most wonderful girl I'll ever know— (WALTER *looks at him in horror and disgust)* She had spirit, brains, looks—everything!

WALTER. Who the hell you talking about?

HILDY. My girl! Who do you think?

WALTER. What are you going to do? Start mumbling about your girl *now?* You got a story to write!

HILDY. I practically told her to go to hell—like she was some waitress!

WALTER. You acted like a man for the first time in your life! *(He crosses to Right)* Don't start crawling now!

HILDY. I'll never love anyone else again! They don't come like that twice in a man's life!

WALTER. You'll sleep it off. Now, listen, Hildy. *(He crosses to window down Right)* I got enough on my mind!

HILDY. When she was sick in the hospital, and you sent me out on the wild goose chase all over Kentucky for three weeks she never even complained—

WALTER. *(Turns—crosses Left)* Ha, ha. Sick in the hospital!

HILDY. Damn it, she was! She nearly died!

WALTER. *(Pacing)* I see. She didn't complain, but she just nearly died! That's all!

HILDY. *(Almost to himself.* WALTER *crosses Center to him)* I would have been on the train now— I would have been—

WALTER. *(Grabbing his arm)* Listen, Hildy. Let me tell you something. *I* was in love once with my—with my—with my third wife. I treated her white—let her have a maid and everything! I was sweet to her!

HILDY. Never mind!

WALTER. I trusted her. *(Pause)* Then I let her meet

a certain party on the *Tribune* and what happened? One night I came home unexpectedly— I let myself in through the bathroom window, and there they were!

HILDY. *(Turning away to typewriter)* I don't want to hear about it.

WALTER. The very next morning, what do I find in the *Tribune,* all over the front page? (WALTER *crosses down Left)* My traction story, I'd been saving for two months! (WALTER *paces up and down Center.)*

HILDY. *(Wheeling on* WALTER) You know a lot about women! You and your stable of tarts! You never met a decent woman! You wouldn't know what to *do* with a pure girl! *(He turns away.)*

WALTER. *(While pacing—wisely)* Oh, yes I would!

HILDY. *(Wheeling back on* WALTER) You take that back!

WALTER. *(Advancing Center, to* HILDY) Say, Hildy, listen! What do you think women are? *Flowers?* Take that dame that shot *(Points finger)* the dentist! And Mrs. Verymilya! Husband comes home all worn out, hungry, takes a spoonful of soup and falls dead! *Arsenic!* And Mrs. Petras! Burning her husband up in a furnace! *(Claps hands)* When you've been in this business as long as I have, you'll know what women are! *(He crosses Right.)*

HILDY. *(Rises, crosses up Left Center)* My God, I'm a sap! Falling for your line of— Naming streets after me!

WALTER. *(Crossing Center to* HILDY) Now, listen, Hildy. You've had a good rest. Get back on the story. That's all you got to do— *(Hands him a pocket flask)* Here. You're just nervous— (WALTER *crosses down Center below table.)*

HILDY. I'll take that— *(Goes to the water cooler. Pouring)* I'll get stewed tonight, and I'm gonna stay stewed for the rest of my life! I'll be a newspaper man! Right in your class! On my pratt in a monke·: cage!

(LOUIE *KNOCKS on door.)*

WALTER. Shut up, you fathead! (HILDY *gestures with his hand and drinks. The KNOCKING continues.* WALTER *pushes* HILDY'S *chair against table, and crossing up Center*) I'll tell you something. If that's Bensinger again, I'm going to crown him, and throw him in the can for keeps! (*At the door*) Who is it?

LOUIE. (*Outside*) Hello, Boss—

WALTER. It's Louie— (*He opens the door.* LOUIE *appears, bearing some evidence of a mishap. His hat is crushed, collar loose.* WALTER *sees this, with alarm*) My God, what's the matter! (WALTER *drags him down Center.*)

HILDY. (*Crossing Center to* LOUIE. *Frantically*) Where's the old lady?

WALTER. What did you do with her?

HILDY. What happened?

WALTER. You been in a fight?

LOUIE. (*Waiting for the barrage of inquiry to subside*) Down Wentworth Avenue. We were going sixty-five miles an hour, you know what I mean?

WALTER. Take the mush out of your mouth!

HILDY. *Where's the old lady!?*

LOUIE. Wait, will you? We run smack into a police patrol. You know what I mean? We broke it in half.

HILDY. Good God! Was she hurt?

WALTER. Where is she? Tell me!

HILDY. For God's sake, Louie!

LOUIE. I'm telling you. Can you imagine bumping into a load of cops? They come rolling out like oranges!

HILDY. (*Seizing him*) What did you do with her, damn you!

WALTER. What became of the old lady, I'm asking you!

LOUIE. Search me. When I come to, I was running down Thirty-fifth Street! Get me?

HILDY. You were with her! You were in the cab, weren't you?

LOUIE. (*Exposing his scalp*) *Was* I! Tony got knocked cold!

(HILDY *crosses down Left.*)

WALTER. *(Crossing up Right)* You God damn butter fingers! I give you an old lady to take somewhere and you hand her over to the cops!

LOUIE. What do you mean, I hand her? The patrol wagon was on the wrong side of the street.

WALTER. *(Turning on* LOUIE*)* That's great! That's perfect! She's probably squawking her head off in some police station. Now everything is fine.

LOUIE. *(Turning away)* I don't think she's talking much, you know what I mean!

HILDY. *(Rushing at* LOUIE*)* Was she killed?

WALTER. *(Crossing down Center to* LOUIE, *smiling)* Was she? Did you notice?

LOUIE. Say, with that alky rap and the bank job and the big blow on my hip! I should stick around asking questions from a lot of cops! *(He crosses up Left Center.)*

HILDY. *(Overcome. He crosses Left to desk)* She's dead! That finishes me!

WALTER. *(Hand in air)* Listen, Hildy. That's Fate. What will be, will be!

HILDY. What am I going to say to Peggy? What'll I tell her?

WALTER. Listen, Hildy! Snap out of it! Would you rather have the old dame dragging the whole police force here?

HILDY. *(Sitting on a table)* I killed her. I did it! Oh, my God, what can I do now? How can I ever face her?

WALTER. *(Becoming the whole Foreign Legion)* Listen, Hildy, if it was my own mother, I'd carry on! For the paper!

HILDY. *(Turning to* LOUIE*)* Where was it? I'll go out!

WALTER. *(Crossing to "Examiner" phone)* You stay here! I'll find out everything right here! *(Into phone.*

HILDY *crosses down Center and sits on table, grabbing phone)* Duffy!—Just a minute— *(To* LOUIE*)* Where was it?

LOUIE. Wentworth and Thirty-fourth—near the corner. (LOUIE *crosses Left. Starts straightening tie and hat.)*

WALTER. *(Into phone)* Call up the Thirty-fifth street station, and ask Nick Gallagher if he's got a report on any old lady that was in a smash-up at Thirty-fourth and Wentworth— *(To* HILDY*)* What's her name?

HILDY. Mrs. Amelia Grant.

WALTER. *(Into phone)* Millie Grant. I don't know! About—fifty-seven? *(With a corroborative look at* HILDY*)* Refined. White hair. Blue eyes. Black cotton stockings. She was wearing rubbers. *(To* HILDY*)* How's that for noticing? *(He crosses up Center. Closes door. Crosses down Right.)*

HILDY. *(In phone)* Gimme an outside wire.

WALTER. Never mind. We'll get the dope *right here.*

*(Another PHONE rings.)*

HILDY. It's that one! (WALTER *starts for "Examiner" phone)* That one! (WALTER *grabs the other phone)* Gimme Wentworth four five five seven!

WALTER. *(Into phone in guarded tone)* Hello— hello— Who? *(Wildly) Hello, Butch! Where are you?*

HILDY. *(Into phone)* Passavant Hospital? Gimme the Receiving Room, will you?

WALTER. Hotel? You mean *you're* in a hotel? What are you doing *there?* Ain't you even *started? ! !*

HILDY. *(Into phone)* Hello, Eddie. Hildy Johnson. Was there an old lady brought in from an auto smash-up—?

WALTER. *(Taking cue, "old lady." Panic)* Oh, for— *(Screaming)* H. Sebastian God! Butch! Listen, it's a matter of life and death, Butch! Listen!

HILDY. *(Into phone)* Nobody?

WALTER. I can't hear you! You got who? Speak up!

HILDY. *(Jiggles hook)* Archer three one two four—

WALTER. A what? ! ! !—Holy God, you can't stop for a dame now!

HILDY. *(Into phone)* Is this the German Deaconess hospital?

WALTER. *(Howling)* I don't care if you've been sweet on her for six *years!* Now, listen, Butch! Our whole lives are at stake! Are you going to let some blonde ruin everything? What do you mean—an hour. It'll be too late in an hour!

HILDY. *(Into phone)* Hello, Max. Hildy Johnson. Was there an old lady from an auto smash-up—?

WALTER. *(Taking cue, "old lady.")* Butch! I'd put my arm in the fire for you up to there! *(Indicates shoulder)* I'd go through hell for you! Now you ain't gonna double-cross me— She does? All right—put her on the wire. I'll talk to her. *Hello!*—Oh, hello, madam! Now listen here, you God damn bum— You can't keep Butch away from his duty! What! What! !—Now, madam! What kind of language is that! Hello—hello!— *(He slams down phone. Grabs "Examiner" phone. Screaming into phone)* Duffy! I'll kill 'em—both of them! I'll butter this town with their brain! Mousing around with some big blonde Annie! *That's* co-operation!

HILDY. *(To WALTER)* Shut up, will you?

WALTER. Duffy!

HILDY. *(Into phone)* You sure? Nobody?

WALTER. *(A howl)* Duffy! *(Slams down phone. Crosses Left.* LOUIE *starts to cross Right)* Louie! It's up to you!

*(They meet just Right of the desk.)*

LOUIE. *(Calmly)* Anything you want.

WALTER. Beat it out and get me hold of some guys, will you?

LOUIE. What do you want?

WALTER. *(Trembling)* Anybody with hair on their chests! Get them off the streets—anywhere—! Offer them anything—only get them! *(Confidentially)* Listen, Louie. We got to get this desk out of here! *(He points to the desk.)*

LOUIE. *(Turning)* This desk?

WALTER. Louie, you're the best friend I got. I'd go through hell for you and I know you won't fail me. *(He pushes* LOUIE *up Center to door)* Get me enough people to move it. Do you understand that? Now, beat it! And remember, I'm relying on you!

LOUIE. *(Departing)* You know me. The shirt off my back.

WALTER. *(Yelling after him)* And Louie! Don't bump into anything! *(He locks the door.)*

HILDY. *(Emotionally, into phone)* Calumet two one hundred—

WALTER. *(Crossing down Left)* That lousy immigrant'll flop on me! I know it. *(Bitterly)* Can you imagine Butch laying up with some fiel at the Revere House! At a time like this! *(He crosses to* HILDY*)* Listen, Hildy— *(Confidentially)* If Louie's not back in five minutes, we'll get it out alone! There's millions of ways! We can start a fire and get the firemen to carry it out in the confusion! *(Crosses up Left Center. Looks at desk.)*

HILDY. Do anything you damn please!—*(Into phone)* Ring that number, will you?

WALTER. We don't even have to do that. We'll get the Chicago Historical Society to claim it as an antique! *(He crosses down Left. Back to audience)* We can move it out in a decent normal manner ourselves! Just the two of us.

HILDY. I don't give a damn what you do!

WALTER. Come on, Hildy! Come here and see if we can move it!

HILDY. Hello! Hello! Is this the Lying-in Hospital? Did you have an auto accident in the last hour?

WALTER. *(Crosses up Left beside desk)* Will you come here?

HILDY. *(Into phone)* Oh, I see. I beg your pardon.

WALTER. *(Turns to* HILDY*)* Right when I'm surrounded, with my back against the wall, you ain't going to let down on me!

HILDY. *(Jiggling the phone hook)* I'm going to lay down on you and spit in your eye, you murderer!

WALTER. *(A step toward Center)* Scared, huh?

HILDY. I don't care what you think! I'm going to find my girl's mother! *(Madly jiggling the hook)* Oh, for God's sake!

WALTER. Your girl! You and Butch McGuirk! Woman lovers!

HILDY. *(Hangs up phone with a bang. He starts up Center)* I'm going to go *out* and find her!

*(At cue, "to go out," comes a loud KNOCK.)*

WALTER. Hey! Don't open that!

HILDY. The hell I won't! I'm going to the morgue! To— Look!—

*(He flings the door open. The* SHERIFF, *accompanied by two deputies,* CARL *and* FRANK—*surrounded by* MCCUE, KRUGER *and* MURPHY, *bar his exit.)*

MURPHY. Oh, there he is!

KRUGER. *(Simultaneously)* Say, Hildy! } *(Together)*

MCCUE. Wait a second—

*(*HILDY *is struggling. The* DEPUTIES *grab him and drag him down Center.* MURPHY *crosses down Right,* MCCUE *stands just Left of* MURPHY, *and* SHERIFF *just to Left of* MCCUE. KRUGER *crosses Right above* WALTER. CARL *is below* HILDY. FRANK *above him.)*

HILDY. Let go of me! What the hell's the big idea?

MURPHY. What's your hurry?
KRUGER. *(Simultaneously)* We want } *(Together.)*
to see you!

HILDY. What are you doing? Take your damn paws
off me!

SHERIFF. Hold him, boys!

WALTER. Who the hell do you think you are, breaking in here like this?

SHERIFF. *(Crossing Left to* WALTER) You can't
bluff me, Burns! I don't care who you are or what
paper you're editor of!

HILDY. Let me go! *(Hysterically)* Let me go! Fellas!
Something's hanged to my girl's mother!

SHERIFF. Hang onto him!

MURPHY. We know what you're up to!

KRUGER. *(Taking cue, "We know")* Going out to get
Williams, probably!

McCUE. *(Taking cue, "going out")* The door was
locked! He and Mollie were talking!

MURPHY. He knows where he is!

HILDY. Listen, guys,—I don't know anything, I tell
you! Hey! Walter! There's been an accident— I just
been calling up the hospitals. I was just going out to
the morgue to see if she was there. Now—

KRUGER. *(Taking cue, "been an accident")* Yeah,
we know all about that.

McCUE. *(Taking cue, "about that")* Yeah!

SHERIFF. *(Taking cue, "morgue")* Johnson, there's
something very, very peculiar going on— *(He crosses
Center towards* HILDY.)

HILDY. Listen, Pinky! You can send somebody with
me if you want to! If you don't believe me!

SHERIFF. I wasn't born yesterday, Johnson. Now
the boys tell me you and Mollie—

HILDY. *(Taking cue, "boys tell me")* Nobody's trying to put anything over on you, Pinky! Now I'm
getting out of here and you can't stop me!

*(He struggles.* FRANK *twists his arm.)*

MURPHY. You're not going anywhere! He's got the story sewed up, Pete. He and his boss. (SHERIFF *crosses to* WALTER) That's why he's here!

WALTER. See here, Hartman! If you've got any accusations to make, make them in the proper manner! Otherwise I'll have to ask you to get out!

SHERIFF. You'll ask me to *what?*

WALTER. *(Pointing to door)* I'll ask you to get out. (WALTER *makes as though to strangle* SHERIFF.)

SHERIFF. Frank, close that door! Don't let anybody in or out!

(FRANK *crosses up Center, closes door. Then back to* HILDY.)

MURPHY. Come on Pinky! Give him a little third degree!

(WALTER *backs Left.*)

SHERIFF. *(Crossing to* HILDY) Johnson, I'm going to the bottom of this! Now then, come clean! What do you know about Williams? Are you going to talk or aren't you?

HILDY. What the hell do I know about Williams?

SHERIFF. All right boys! Take him along. (FRANK *and* CARL *drag* HILDY *up Center)* I got ways of making him talk. (HILDY *struggles.)*   } *(Together.)*

HILDY. Look out—you—!

McCUE. *(As* HILDY *struggles)* What's the use of fighting, Hildy?

(FRANK *pulls gun from pocket, hands it to* CARL.)

HILDY. Say what's the idea?
CARL. He's got a gun on him!
HILDY. No, you don't! Hey, Walter!   } *(Together.)*
WALTER. What is it? Here!
SHERIFF. Gimme that! *(Takes the gun.)*

MURPHY. Jesse James, huh! The drugstore cowboy!

McCUE. *(Taking cue, "Jesse James, huh!")* He's been going to the movies. Two-gun Johnson!

KRUGER. *(Taking cue, "he's been going")* The terror of Wilson Avenue beach!

(KRUGER *crosses slowly to cooler, Left.)*

SHERIFF. *(Frozen, looking at the gun)* Where did you get this?

HILDY. I got a right to carry a gun if I want to.

SHERIFF. Not this gun!

WALTER. Now see here, Hartman! I can explain that. He was having some trouble with the Durkin story— (HILDY *motions* WALTER *to be still)* and I give it to him—to defend himself!

SHERIFF. Oh, you did! Well, that's very, very interesting! This *happens* to be the gun that Earl Williams shot his way out with!

McCUE. What? What's that?⎫
KRUGER. So that's it, is it? ⎬ *(Together.)*
MURPHY. Oh ho! ⎭

WALTER. *(At climax of noise. To* SHERIFF) Are you trying to make me out a liar?

SHERIFF. *(Wildly)* I know my own gun, don't I? *(He realizes his error. Turns away.)*

MURPHY. I knew something stunk⎫
around here. ⎪
McCUE. *(Taking cue, "stunk")* ⎬ *(Together.)*
*That's* what it was! ⎪
MURPHY. *(Bitterly to* HILDY) Getting⎪
married! ⎭

KRUGER. Yeah. Maybe Willams was gonna be his best man.

SHERIFF. *(Coming out of a trance. To* HILDY) Where is he? Where you got him?

WALTER. You're barking up the wrong tree, Hartman—

SHERIFF. *(Crossing Left Center to* WALTER*)* I'll give you three minutes to tell me where he is!

HILDY. He went over to the hospital to call on Professor Eglehofer!

SHERIFF. *(Turning to* HILDY*)* What!!

HILDY. With a bag of marshmallows! *(The* SHERIFF *crosses down Right Center, then turns and crosses Left to the door.)*

WALTER. Take a magazine along—

MURPHY. Come on, Hildy! Where is he?

McCUE. That's a fine trick, Hildy. I thought we were friends.

SHERIFF. *(Rushing back from the toilet. He crosses Left Center to* WALTER*)* By God, I'll show you!

MURPHY. *(Crossing Center to* WALTER*)* Look here, Pete! What about Mr. Burns? Ask the Master Mind!

McCUE. Yeah. What's *he* doing over here?

SHERIFF. *(Grabbing* WALTER'S *arm)* Speak up, Burns! What do you know about this?

WALTER. *(Gently, but firmly, disengaging his arm)* Listen Hartman— *(He crosses Left to swivel chair.)*

MURPHY. The hell with that! *(He turns to* HILDY*)* Where is he?

WALTER. *(As he sits)* The *Examiner* is not obstructing justice or aiding criminals. You ought to know that!

McCUE. *(Pointing to the "Examiner" phone)* Look! Somebody was talking on there! The receiver is off! *(*McCUE *jumps for the phone)* I'll find out who it is.

SHERIFF. *(Also jumping)* Leave that alone! I'm in charge here! *(He crosses Right.)*

HILDY. Walter, listen! If I don't get out of here—

SHERIFF. Quiet, everybody! I'll handle this. *(To* McCUE*)* It may be Earl Williams.

HILDY. Tell him to come on over.

SHERIFF. Sssh! *(Into phone, elaborately disguising his voice)* Hello, Earl?

WALTER. Scotland Yard.

SHERIFF. *(To* McCUE, *in a whisper)* Trace this call

—quick! (McCue *jumps for another phone*) Yes, this is Walter.

McCue. *(Into another phone)* Trace the call on twenty-one. Hurry it, please.

Sheriff. *(Into phone)* What? You gotta go where? Who is this?

Walter. You're talking to the *Examiner*, Hawkshaw!

McCue. That's right, Sheriff!

Sheriff. *(Puts down phone. Crossing to* Walter) Johnson, you're under arrest! You too, Burns!

Walter. *(Rising)* Who's under arrest? Listen, you pimple head, do you realize what you're doing?

Sheriff. *(To* Carl) Get the Mayor, Carl! Ask him to come over here! *(To* Walter) We'll see about this!

*(As* Carl *goes to the telephone the door opens and* Mrs. Grant *enters with* Two Policemen.)

First Policeman. *(Entering)* —in here, Madam?

*(*First Policeman *crosses down Right Center.* Second Policeman *stands by door.)*

Hildy. *(Leaping forward happily)*  
Mother! ⎫  
Mrs. Grant. *(Crossing Center)* That ⎬ *(Together.)*  
man there! With the grey necktie! ⎭

*(She points accusing finger at* Walter. Walter *backs down Left.)*

Hildy. Mother! Oh, my God, I'm so glad to see you! Are you all right? Tell me.

Sheriff. *(Taking cue, "oh, my God!")* What's the idea here?

Policeman. *(Taking cue, "idea here")* This lady claims she was kidnapped!

Sheriff. What!

MRS. GRANT. They dragged me all the way down the stairs— I'm black and blue all over! Then they ran into an automobile and I was nearly killed!

SHERIFF. Just a minute! What did this man have to do with it, Lady?

MRS. GRANT. He was the one in charge of everything! He told them to kidnap me.

(MURPHY *comes Right.*)

WALTER. *(Crossing up Center)* Are you referring to me, Madam?

HILDY. Mother—listen!

MRS. GRANT. *(To* WALTER) You know you did! You told them to take me out of here!

SHERIFF. *(To* WALTER) What about this, Burns! Kidnapping, eh?  *(Together.)*

WALTER. It's beyond me! Who is this woman?

(KRUGER *crosses down Left.*)

MRS. GRANT. Oh! Oh, what a thing to say! I was standing right here— *(Points up Left Center)* after the girl jumped out of that window!

MURPHY. That's right, Pinkey!

McCUE. I saw her!

HILDY. Mother, for God's sake!  *(Together.)*

CARL. Right!

SHERIFF. *(To* CARL) Did you get the Mayor? Was he in? *(He crosses up Center.)*

CARL. He's coming over. (SHERIFF *crosses down Center to Right of* MRS. GRANT.)

WALTER. *(Taking cue, "Get the Mayor." He crosses Center and grabs* MRS. GRANT's *arm)* Now, Madam, be honest, if you were out joy-riding—drunk! And got in some scrape—why don't you admit it, instead of accusing—

(CARL *crosses Right behind* HILDY.)

MRS. GRANT. *(Taking cue, "Admit")* You ruffians!
*(She pounds his chest edging* WALTER *up Left to desk)*
You unprincipled man! How dare you say a thing like
that! *(She crosses Center to* SHERIFF.)

HILDY. Please, Mother! He's just crazy!—Don't!

MRS. GRANT. *(Continues speech)* I'll tell you something more, Officer! I'll tell you why they did it! I was
in here and they had some kind of a murderer—
hiding him!

SHERIFF. Hiding him, hiding him! In here!

MURPHY. Hiding him where—

HILDY. Mother!

McCUE. Where was he? Where did *(Together.)*
they have him?

KRUGER. Hiding him right in this
room.

WALTER. *(Pounding desk three times)* Madam,
you're a God damn liar! *(He ad libs. Pointing at* MRS.
GRANT.)

McCUE. For God's sake, tell us where
he was!

MURPHY. Did they tell you they were *(Together.)*
hiding him? Where was he?

KRUGER. For God's sake tell us, where
is he?

SHERIFF. *(Through the medley, pounding three times
on the desk)* Shut up, everybody! *(There are three answering knocks from the desk.* WALTER *grabs his head
and turns away.* SHERIFF *and* POLICEMEN *get guns)*
What was that?

MRS. GRANT. *(Advancing to Right of desk)* That's
it.

McCUE. He's in the desk!

MURPHY. For the love of—

KRUGER. Holy God, he's in there!

SHERIFF. Aha! I thought so! *(He* *(Together.)*
crosses down to Left Center)* Stand
back, everybody! He's in there all right!

FRANK. Look out, Sheriff! He may shoot!

WALTER. *(Crossing to* MRS. GRANT) You grey haired old Judas!

MRS. GRANT. *(Exiting)* Oh dear! Oh dear!

SHERIFF. Get your guns, everybody!

(FRANK *crosses to Left of desk.*)

HILDY. He's harmless, for God's sake! What's the idea!

(McCUE *crosses to his table.*)

SHERIFF. Don't take any chances. Shoot right through the desk!

HILDY. *(Crossing Center)* Don't do that! He isn't armed!

MURPHY. *(Phone)* City desk! Quick!

SHERIFF. *(To* SECOND POLICEMAN) Close the door. You stand there! *(To* FIRST POLICEMAN) You cover the windows. *(Indicates with his gun.* HILDY *backs up Center.)*    *(Together.)*

MURPHY. Look out where you're pointing that gun, Pinkey!

McCUE. *(Into phone)* Gimme Emil!

KRUGER. *(Phone)* Gimme the City desk!

MURPHY. Hold the wire! I've got a flash for you.    *(Together.)*

SHERIFF. Now then! Everybody aim right at the center.

HILDY. You can't hurt anybody! That's murder.

SHERIFF. Carl! Frank! One of you get on each side of the desk. (CARL *crosses to Right of desk)* Now then, I'm going to count three.

MURPHY. *(Phoning in the silence)* I'll have it in a minute—

SHERIFF. One!

KRUGER. Right away now!
SHERIFF. Two!

(LOUIE *enters, accompanied by two people he has picked up in the streets. One is a* COLORED BOY *in short pants, the second is a* SAILOR. *They advance down Center. See crowd, stop.*)

POLICEMAN. *(At door, opposing them)* Hey, what do you want?

(WALTER *and* HILDY *push him out.* LOUIE *and his assistants turn and rush out.*)

SHERIFF. *(Crossing up Center. Wheeling)* Who was that?
WALTER. Double-crossing Sicilian!

(WALTER *crosses Right; looks at* HILDY. HILDY *crosses down Center.*)

SHERIFF. Shut up!
KRUGER. *(Again sneaks up on the desk. Into phone)* Keep holding it!
SHERIFF. Now then! Keep everybody out of here! I want quiet!—*(He crosses down Center)* There's a dozen guns on you, Williams! (WALTER *grabs "Examiner" phone*) Do you surrender or not?
WALTER. Duffy Cornell!
SHERIFF. Are you ready, boys?
CARL. Yeh—
SHERIFF. All right. Now everybody aim right at the center. Now then—up with it!

(CARL *and* FRANK *raise the cover. The* SHERIFF *waits a discreet distance, until he sees there is no danger.* WILLIAMS *is cowering in the desk, his hands over his face.*)

WILLIAMS. Go on—shoot me!
SHERIFF. Got you, Williams!

*(The* DEPUTIES *grab him, drag him up Center. The* TWO POLICEMEN *cross up Center.)*

DEPUTIES. Grab him, there! That's him! That's him! Don't let him shoot! Stick 'em up! You! (Two POLICEMEN *drag him out. The* SHERIFF *follows.* CARL *and* FRANK *stand each side of the door)* Clout him! Give him the boots! Hold his arms!

MURPHY. *(Taking cue, "Shoot me")* Earl Wiliams was just captured in the press room o' the Criminal Court building hiding in a desk.

McCUE. *(Taking cue, "Shoot me")* The Sheriff just caught Williams in a roll top right here in the room.

KRUGER. *(Taking cue, "Shoot me")* Just nabbed Williams hiding in a desk, criminal court press room.

McCUE. *(Continuous speech)* Williams put up a desperate struggle but the police overpowered him.

MURPHY. *(Taking cue, "desperate struggle")* Williams tried to shoot it out with the cops but his gun wouldn't work.

KRUGER. *(Taking cue, "out with the cops." Into phone)* Williams was unconscious when they opened the desk—

WALTER. Duffy! The *Examiner* just turned Earl Williams over to the Sheriff—

SHERIFF. *(Coming into room)* Just a minute! Put the cuffs on those two. *(Indicating* HILDY) Harboring a fugitive from justice!

(CARL *and* FRANK *put cuffs on* HILDY *and* WALTER.)

MURPHY. *(Into phone)* A well dressed society woman tipped off the cops. Call you back in a minute—

KRUGER. *(Taking cue, "tipped off the cops")* An old sweetheart of Williams double-crossed him— Call you back—

*(Sheriff crosses Left Center.)*

McCue. *(Taking cue, "double crossed him")* More in a minute.

Murphy. Where's that old lady?

McCue. Hey, madam—     *(Together.)*

Kruger. Wait a minute— Where's that old dame?

*(They exit in a hurry.)*

Sheriff. *(Into McCue's phone)* Hello, girlie! Gimme Jacobi! Quick!—

Walter. Hartman— You're going to wish for the rest of your life you'd never been born!

*(The Mayor enters. He crosses Center.)*

Mayor. Fine work, Pete! You certainly delivered the goods! I'm proud of you.

*(Carl crosses up Center beside door.)*

Sheriff. *(Over his shoulder as he phones)* Look kind of natural, don't they, Fred? *(Referring to the handcuffs.)*

Mayor. A sight for sore eyes! Well, it looks like you boys stepped in something up to your neck!

Hildy. *(A step Center)* Go on! Laugh!

Mayor. That's pretty, isn't it? Aiding an escaped criminal, huh?

Sheriff. And a little charge of kidnapping I'm looking into! *(Into phone)* That's the jail. There must be somebody over there!

Mayor. Well! Looks like about ten years apiece for you birds.

Walter. Does it? Well, whenever you think you've got the *Examiner* licked that's a good time to get out of town.

HILDY. On a hand-car!

MAYOR. Whistling in the dark, eh? Well, it isn't going to help you. You're through. *(Crosses down Left.)*

WALTER. Yeah? The last man that told me that was Barney Schmidt, a week before he cut his throat.

MAYOR. Is that so?

WALTER. And remember George T. Yorke, biowing his head off with a shot-gun? We've been in worse jams than this—haven't we, Hildy? Something seems to watch over the *Examiner*.

HILDY. Yeah. When that minister sued us—remember? *(Indicates cuffs)* False arrest?

WALTER. Oh, yes— *(To the* MAYOR*)* The Reverend J. B. Godolphin sued the *Examiner* once for—a hundred thousand dollars. It seems that we'd called him a fairy. Well, the day of the trial came and the Reverend was on his way to court—

HILDY. With all his lawyers and medical witnesses!

WALTER. Drowned. by God! Drowned in the river! With their automobile and law books and affidavits and everything! And I got the same feeling right now that I had five minutes before that accident!

MAYOR. Very amusing, but somehow I don't seem to be frightened.

SHERIFF. I never felt better in my life. *(Into phone)* Jacobi?—I caught him— Williams. Single-handed— Yeah. They're bringing him right over. Notify everybody. We're to proceed with the hanging per schedule. *(Wiggles telephone for another call.)*

WALTER. You're going to be in office for exactly two days more and then we're setting you out on your—

SHERIFF. Give me the state's attorney's office.

HILDY. *(Edging Center)* And when you're walking up and down North Avenue with blue eye glasses selling lead pencils, we're not going to forget you, either!

SHERIFF. We're going to be selling lead pencils, eh?

MAYOR. Don't even answer him.

SHERIFF. *(Into phone)* Hello. Prystalski? This is

Hartman. Come right over to my office, will you? I've just arrested a couple of important birds. I want you to take their confessions. *(Hangs up.)*

WALTER. *(Leaning far over table to "Examiner" phone)* Duff! Get Clarence Darrow!

MAYOR. Get anybody you want! All the Darrows in the world aren't going to help you!

WALTER. *(Counting on fingers)* Schmidt, Yorks, Godolphin. *(Pointing)* You're next, Fred.

MAYOR. The power of the press, huh? Well, it don't scare me! Not an iota!

SHERIFF. Just a couple of windbags! (PINCUS *reels on, stewed, waving reprieve)* That's all they are! Take 'em along, Carl!

PINCUS. Here's your reprieve.

MAYOR. *(Crossing up Center)* Get out of here!

PINCUS. You can't bribe me!

SHERIFF. Get out of here, you!

PINCUS. *(Gives it to* MAYOR*)* I won't. Here's your reprieve!

HILDY. *(Grabbing* PINCUS*)* What's that?

WALTER. Reprieve?

PINCUS. I don't want to be City Sealer.

MAYOR. Who is this man?

SHERIFF. *(Frenzied)* Throw him out, Frank!

(FRANK *grabs* PINCUS.)

HILDY. *(Seizing* PINCUS *with his free hand)* Who was bribing you?

PINCUS. They wouldn't take it!—

MAYOR. *(Crossing down Left)* You're insane!

WALTER. Wait a minute! What's your name?

PINCUS. *(Being pulled apart)* Irving Pincus!

HILDY. *(Throws* FRANK'S *arm off* PINCUS*)* Wait a minute. Let go there!

WALTER. Murder, huh?

HILDY. Hanging an innocent man to win an election!

SHERIFF. That's a lie!

(FRANK *backs up Center.*)

MAYOR. I never saw him before in my life!

WALTER. *(To* PINCUS) When did you deliver it first?

HILDY. Who did you talk to?

PINCUS. They started right in bribing me!

HILDY. Who's "they?"

PINCUS. *(Indicating)* Them!

MAYOR. That's absurd on the face of it, Mr. Burns! He's talking like a child!

WALTER. Yeah?

MAYOR. Certainly! Why, if this unfortunate man Williams has really been reprieved, I personally am tickled to death! Aren't you, Pete?

HILDY. Go on, you'd kill your Mother to get elected, and you know it!

MAYOR. *(Crossing up Center)* That's a terrible thing to say, Johnson, about anybody! Now, look here, Walter, you're an intelligent man—

WALTER. *(Stopping the* MAYOR) Just a minute. *(To* PINCUS) All right, Mr. Pincus. Let's have your story.

PINCUS. Well, I've been married for nineteen years—

WALTER. Well, just skip all that.

MAYOR. *(Loudly)* Take those handcuffs off the boys, Pete. That wasn't at all necessary—

SHERIFF. *(Springing to obey. He crosses Right behind* PINCUS) I was just going to—

MAYOR. I can't tell you how badly I feel about this, Walter. There was no excuse for Hartman flying off the handle.

SHERIFF. *(Busy with the handcuffs)* I was only doing my duty. There wasn't anything personal.

HILDY. Give me a drink, Walter.

WALTER. Over there!

(HILDY *walks over to the water cooler as the* MAYOR *continues.*)

MAYOR. Sheriff— *(He is looking over the reprieve)* This document is authentic! Earl Williams, thank God, has been reprieved, and the commonwealth of Chicago has been spared the painful necessity of shedding blood.

(SHERIFF *stands Right of* WALTER.)

WALTER. Save that for the *Tribune.*
MAYOR. What did you say your name was—Pincus?
PINCUS. That's right. *(Shows a locket)* Here's a picture of the wife.
MAYOR. *(Trapped)* A very fine-looking woman.
PINCUS. She's good enough for me.
HILDY. I'll bet she is.

(PEGGY *enters. Crosses Left below desk.*)

MAYOR. A real character.
PEGGY. Hildy, what's the matter? What are they going to do? Mother said—
HILDY. Peggy, don't bawl me out now.
WALTER. Nobody's going to do anything.
MAYOR. *(Crosses Right to* WALTER) Of course not. My good friend Walter Burns and I understand each other perfectly, I trust.
SHERIFF. And so do I.
MAYOR. So do you what, you God damn hoodoo! (SHERIFF *exits.* FRANK *follows.*) And now, Mr. Pincus, if you'll come with us, we'll take you over to the Warden's office and deliver the reprieve.

(MAYOR *and* PINCUS *cross up Center.*)

PEGGY. Hildy, Mother said that they'd arrested you—
PINCUS. *(In door)* If I was to go home and tell my wife—

MAYOR. *(Pushing him out)* The hell with your wife.

*(They exit.)*

PINCUS. But she loves me.

(CARL *exits, closing door.*)

WALTER. *(Facing front)* Wait till those two Greeks read the *Examiner* tomorrow! Hildy, I'll tell you what I want you to do.

(PEGGY *turns and faces* WALTER.)

HILDY. What?

WALTER. *(Crossing Center)* I want you to get this guy Pincus over to the office tomorrow—

(PEGGY *stops him. He tips hat.*)

HILDY. *(Sitting in swivel chair)* Nothing doing, Walter. I'm all washed up. I mean it this time, Walter.

PEGGY. *(To* HILDY) Oh, Hildy, if I only thought you did.

HILDY. Listen, Peggy—if I'm not telling you the absolute truth may God strike me dead right now. I'm going to New York with you tonight— If you give me this one last chance! I'll cut out drinking and swearing and everything connected with the God damn newspaper business. I won't even read a newspaper. This time I'm through, and I mean it. I know I don't deserve you, Peggy. I've done everything in the world to prove that, I guess.

PEGGY. *(Crosses Left. Kneeling by* HILDY) Darling, don't talk that way. I want you just the way you are, anyway.

WALTER. *(Crossing Left behind* HILDY) Hildy, I didn't know it was anything like this. Why didn't you say so? I'd be the last person in the world to want to come between you and your happiness.

HILDY. *(Staggered. Looks at* WALTER. PEGGY *rises, backs Center)* What?

WALTER. You ought to know that— *(He pushes his head away)* I love you, you crazy Swede! *(To* PEGGY) You're getting a great guy, Peggy!

HILDY. Never mind the Valentines. (HILDY *rises. Holds out hand)* Good-bye, you lousy bohunk—

WALTER. You're a great newspaperman, Hildy. I'm sorry to see you go—damn sorry.

HILDY. Well, if I ever come back to the business— *(To* PEGGY) Which I won't— *(To* WALTER, *his arm around* PEGGY) There's only one man I'd work for. You know that, don't you?

WALTER. *(Shaking his fist)* I'd kill you if you ever worked for anybody else.

HILDY. Hear that, Peggy? That's my diploma. *(He hesitates, turns to* WALTER) Well, Walter— I don't know what to say— *(To* PEGGY) Twelve years we've been knocking around together—before you were born— *(To* WALTER) Remember that time we had to keep that bigamist under cover? *(To* PEGGY) We hid in the sauerkraut factory.

WALTER. *(To* PEGGY) Yeah! And Peggy, get him to tell you sometime about the Haggerty poisoning, when we stole old lady Haggerty's stomach right out from under the coroner's nose!

HILDY. *(Delighted, to* PEGGY) We had to hide for a week, the two of us.

PEGGY. Darling—

HILDY. *(Back to life)* What?

PEGGY. You don't want to go to New York—down deep.

HILDY. Aw, kiddo—what do you mean? I was just talking. *(With a nervous laugh)* I'd feel worse if I stayed, I guess—

PEGGY. Hildy, if I thought you were going to be un-happy— I mean, if you really wanted to—

WALTER. *(To* PEGGY) I wouldn't let him stay— Go on, Hildy, before I make you City Editor.

HILDY. Hurry up, Peggy. He means it. (HILDY *crosses up Left Center. Puts on hat.)*

WALTER. Any objection to my kissing the bride?

(PEGGY *crosses up Center.)*

HILDY. *(Stopping)* It's O.K. with me. *(He looks at* PEGGY. *She smiles)* Go ahead, Mrs. Johnson.

(WALTER *crosses Center.* PEGGY *comes down Center.)*

WALTER. *(Removing his hat and kissing her suddenly on the lips)* Thank you—what time does your train go?

(HILDY *has coat on arm. Comes down Center.)*

PEGGY. *(Taking* HILDY's *arm)* There's another one at 12:40.

WALTER. New York Central, eh? *(He takes out watch. To* HILDY) I wish there was time to get you a little wedding present—but it's awful short notice.

PEGGY. *(Straining to be gone)* Thank you, Mr. Burns, but Hildy's all the wedding present I want— *(Laughing a little)* If I've really got him.

HILDY. *(Puts his arm around her)* Ah, forget it, Walter.

WALTER. *(Fingering watch)* Hold on! I want you to have something to remember me by. You can't just leave like this— Here! *(He holds out watch.)*

HILDY. *(Embarrassed)* Gee, no, Walter. You just make me feel like a—

WALTER. *(With affected brusqueness)* Shut up! You're going to take it, I tell you! It was a present from the Big Chief himself! And if you'll look inside— *(Opening the watch)* You'll find a little inscription. "To the Best Newspaperman I know"— When you get to New York you can scratch out my name and put yours in its place, if you want to— I kinda hope you won't—                                *(WARN Curtain.)*

HILDY. You know I wouldn't do that—

WALTER. Here.

*(Giving him the watch. HILDY takes it. WALTER pats him on the shoulder, his face averted.)*

HILDY. *(Crosses up Center, gets suitcase)* Well, this is the first and last thing I ever got from a news-paper—

PEGGY. *(Crossing Left Center to WALTER. Shakes hands)* Good-bye, Mr. Burns— I always had a queer opinion of you, Mr. Burns. I still think you're a little peculiar, but you're all right underneath. I mean I think you're a peach.

WALTER. So are you! You look just like a little flower! *(He turns away up Left.)*

*(PEGGY crosses up Center.)*

HILDY. *(Ushering PEGGY out)* Good-bye, you big baboon—

PEGGY. Good-bye—

*(They exit.)*

WALTER. *(Calling after them, leaning against the door)* Good-bye, Johnson! Be good to yourself—and the little girl—

HILDY'S VOICE. The same to you and many of them!

PEGGY. Good-bye.

WALTER. *(WALTER waits till HILDY and PEGGY are out of sight and earshot. He stands dejectedly leaning against Center. He walks slowly to the "Examiner" phone. The receiver is still off the hook, the obedient DUFFY still on the other end. WALTER hesitates sentimentally, the receiver in his hand. Then he heaves a huge sigh and speaks)* Duffy!—*(He sounds a bit tired)* Listen. I want you to send a wire to the Chief of Police at La Porte, Indiana— That's right— Tell him to meet the twelve-forty out of Chicago— New York Central—and arrest Hildy Johnson and bring him back here. Wire him a full description. The son of a bitch stole my watch!

CURTAIN

THE END

# THE FRONT PAGE

## PROPERTY PLOTS

### Act I

Windows
    Cut glass
    Fix height (as marked)
    Fix shades (as marked)
    Fix shade string (Up stage window)
Table—Right Center
    Telephones (2 tele-       Cards
      phones painted red.    Papers
      *Examiner* phones)    Cigarettes
    4 chairs             Money
    Stool
Table—Up Center
    Paper in typewriter
    Pile of written paper
    Matches
    Paper key down
Desk—Open
    Atomizer, cotton, pencil, telephone (with glass
      mouthpiece)

| Left drawers | Right - upper drawer | Right - |
|---|---|---|
| Drawers | Scripts | lower drawer |
| Shirt | Hot water bottle | Red Cross stuff |
| Pie | Paper | |

Spittoon—Down stage Right
Scrap Basket—In front of desk chair
Magazine—Off Left
Fire Bell—On back wall
Mirror—On Left wall

## Act II

Fix windows
Fix shades
Try blackout
Glass out
Mattress for MOLLIE
Strike gallows
Guns for shot (2)
Close desk
Strike MURPHY'S chair
  (Center)
Stool under table
Telephone on top of desk
Cotton and atomizer on
  desk
Test door

Reprieve for PINCUS
Suitcase for PEGGY
Money for LOUIE
Jail lights on
Gun for EARL WILLIAMS
Card for MAYOR
Fix KRUGER's chair
Paper for HILDY to fold
  (on McCUE's table)
Paper and pencil for
  HILDY (on table Right
  Center)
Door Right Center—Open
Door Left—Ajar

## Act III

Paper on table
Telephone off hook
Doors closed
Shades pulled
Guns for POLICEMAN
Guns for SHERIFF

Reprieve
Handcuffs
Lights on
  Right
  Left

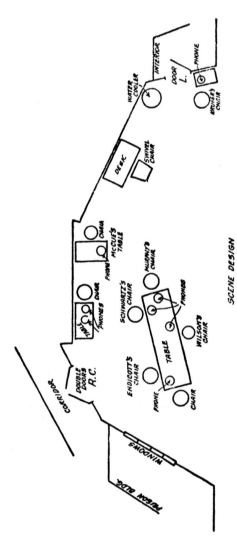

SCENE DESIGN

"THE FRONT PAGE"